Most believers never learn th€
salvation of the spirit unto eterna
(sanctification) unto reward. Jim Harman clearly distinguishes
between the two in his excellent volume, *Salvation of the Soul*.
Understanding this truth is indispensable for preparing to meet
Jesus at the Judgment Seat of Christ. I am so thankful for
Brother Harman's excellent resource that rightly divides the
Scriptures.

James S. Hollandsworth, pastor
Author of *The End of the Pilgrimage*
www.KingdomPreparation.com

Having just read Jim Harman's *Salvation of the Soul*, I find it
to be one of the most provocative and thoughtful presentations I
have ever read on the distinctive differences of soul and spirit
salvation. I highly commend it for personal study and
edification. You will be blessed.

Jim Henry – Pastor Emeritus
First Baptist Orlando, Orlando, FL

Jim Harman's work on the salvation of the soul is greatly
needed and his burden for "souls" is evident. This book, in a
concise manner, shows the believer how their soul can be saved.
Jim explains how salvation of the soul is only applicable to
believers and is a product of sanctification. He rightly divides
the gift of God, which is absent from works, and the reward of
God, which is according to works. His focus upon on the Word
of God is refreshing. His willingness to let the Word speak is
brave. So many preach what they have always been taught or
understood and are unwilling to examine the potential that what
they have been taught is wrong. Not so with Jim's book
*Salvation of the Soul*. Jim brings great light on this many times
wrongly understood subject.

Scott Crawford – Ashville, NC
Author of *Perseverance Pays: Winning
the Crown of Life*
www.Wordoftruthclass.org

*Salvation of the Soul* clearly expresses *one of the most critical messages* specifically directed for God's children. By properly understanding the *complete tripartite salvation message*, specifically the difference between two of its parts – spirit and soul, you will not only be able to see the harmony in Scripture, but you will also be in a position of achieving the abundant, overcoming life God desires, which will maturate in Christ's soon-coming Millennial Kingdom.

Charles Strong – Harlingen, TX
www.Bibleone.net

*Salvation of the Soul* needs to be read by every Christian. Few in the body of Christ are aware of the important truths that are shared in this book. Whether you act on the exhortative teaching will determine whether you rule and reign with Jesus or whether you suffer loss at the Judgment Seat of Christ.

Daniel Rydstedt – Springfield, MO
Author of *Be the Bride Series*
www.rapturebrideprophecy.com

James Harman's new book gives believers a desperately needed "wake-up call." Most have been deluded into thinking that the message of salvation is simply a "heaven or hell" choice. *Salvation of the Soul* will help you see what is at stake when we stand before the Judgment Seat of Christ. Those who are faithful will be wonderfully blessed, while those believers who are not living in whole-hearted discipleship will suffer great loss. Let us be sober and ready for that coming day.

Tom Finley – Oakboro, NC
Author of *The Victorious Christian Life*
www.seekersofchrist.org

# Salvation of the Soul

HOW STANDING BEFORE CHRIST
CAN BE OUR MOST GLORIOUS MOMENT

## James T. Harman

**Prophecy
Countdown
Publications**

# Salvation of the Soul

Copyright © 2019, James T. Harman

Prophecy Countdown Publications, LLC
P.O. Box 941612
Maitland, FL 32794
www.ProphecyCountdown.com

ISBN: 978-1-7332995-0-3

All references from Scripture are from the New King James Version unless noted otherwise:

| | | |
|---|---|---|
| AMP | Amplified Bible, copyright ©1987 Lockman Foundation | |
| ESV | English Standard Version®, copyright ©2001 Crossway | |
| KJV | King James Version, copyright ©1982 | |
| NASB | New American Standard Bible, copyright ©1960 | |
| NIV | New International Version, copyright ©2011 | |
| NLT | New Living Translation, copyright ©1996 | |
| YLT | Young's Literal Translation, copyright ©1898 | |

Scripture abbreviations as used throughout this book are from the *Blue Letter Bible* (www.BlueLetterBible.org), and they are summarized on p. 55. Numerical references to selected words in the text of Scripture are from James H. Strong's dictionaries of Hebrew and Greek words.

Words in bold emphasis are the author's and not in original Scripture. Certain words such as *Kingdom* and *Judgment Seat of Christ* are capitalized to emphasize their importance but not in accordance with traditional fashions. Emphasis added in quoted material and Scripture are the author's unless noted otherwise.

Cover image of the Holy City by Steve Creitz, www.ProphecyArt.com
Back cover image of bride by Kume Bryant, www.kumebryant.com

---

**NOTE TO READER**
The objective of this writing is to provide readers with a better understanding of the salvation spoken of in the book of Hebrews: "*How shall we escape if we neglect so great a salvation*"(Heb 2:3). The purpose of this book is to expound the subject of the salvation of the soul, which has been greatly neglected by the modern church. Throughout this book, bibliographical references may be provided in the comments on selected texts with the commentator's last name along with page numbers (in parentheses) for the references cited.

# Prologue

In the fall of 2017, I was fortunate to visit the land of Israel with Pastor Jim Henry's final tour of the Holy Lands, and I was blessed to walk many of the places where our Lord carried out His ministry. When we visited the traditional site for the Sermon on the Mount,[1] Pastor Henry had everyone in our group read one verse from this famous sermon. When it came to my turn, I read the following: *"Therefore you shall be perfect, just as your Father in heaven is perfect"* (Mat 5:48).

Oswald Chambers explains this passage concisely:

> The perfection of v. 48 refers to the disposition of God in me—'Ye shall be perfect as your Father in heaven is perfect' (R.V.) not in a future state, but – You shall be perfect as your Father in heaven is perfect if you let Me work that perfection in you. If the Holy Spirit has transformed you on the inside, you will exhibit not good human characteristics, but divine characteristics in a human being (Chambers, p. 40).

The standards set by Jesus in the Sermon on the Mount can only be achieved by allowing Jesus to control our lives in our daily walk with Him. By doing this, we can grow into the mature and complete believers of whom Christ speaks. The Amplified version describes it as follows:

*You, therefore, must be perfect [growing into complete maturity of godliness in mind and character, having reached the proper height of virtue and integrity], as your heavenly Father is perfect.* (Mat 5:48 – AMP) [Lev 19:2, 18]

The faith Jesus desires His disciples to realize is mature and complete, reflecting the heavenly Father's character, which embodies holiness and love. While we will never be as perfect as God the Father during our current pilgrimage, Jesus was exhorting His disciples to strive to be godlike in character and actions. While perfection is not something we will obtain in this life, He wants us to rely on His presence in our lives:

*I have been crucified with Christ; it is no longer I who live, but Christ lives in me; and the life which I now live in the flesh I live by faith in the Son of God, who loved me and gave Himself for me.* (Gal 2:20)

By allowing Christ to control our lives we can develop into the complete and mature people He wants us to be. Becoming *perfect* through Christ's presence is what this study is all about.

The salvation of the soul is probably one of the most misunderstood concepts in the Church today. Most people think that the salvation of the spirit and the salvation of the soul are the same thing even though the Scriptures tell us something different.

The salvation of a person's spirit is very simple. Acts 16:30-31 tells us: *"30) 'Sirs, what must I do to be saved?' 31)...So they said, 'Believe on the Lord Jesus Christ, and you will be saved, you and your household.'"* The salvation of the spirit is based on the finished work of our Saviour Jesus Christ at Calvary – the spirit is saved simply by believing on the Lord Jesus Christ. While the spirit is saved by faith in Christ, the soul is being saved based upon the faithfulness of the believer. The salvation of the soul will ultimately be determined when Christ returns:

*5) This salvation, which is ready to be revealed on the last day for all to see...9) receiving the end of your faith—the salvation of your souls.* (1Pe 1:5 – NLT, 9)

The purpose of this brief study is to help you prepare for the moment when you stand before Christ on that last day.

# Dedication

---

For all those
who love His appearing

---

*There is laid up for me the **crown of righteousness**,*
*which the Lord, the righteous Judge,*
*will give to me on that Day,*
*and not to me only but also*
***to all who have loved His appearing**.*
(2Ti 4:8)

---

*Looking for that blessed hope,*
*and the glorious appearing*
*of the great God and*
*our Saviour Jesus Christ.*
(Titus 2:13 – KJV)

*That the trial of your faith being much more precious
than gold that perisheth, though it be tried by fire, might
be found unto praise and honor and glory at the
appearing of Jesus Christ* (1Pe 1:7).

The salvation of the soul is a continuous work of the
Lord in the lives of all believers. And in order to have a
saved soul, one must have a matured faith. Since the
believer's faith cannot be matured unless it overcomes
the trials of this world, God then, in loving care allows
certain trials to come into the believer's life. And as the
believer overcomes these by faith, new and more intense
trials are ordered by God so that the maturing faith may
continue to grow (Whipple, p. 63).

*If anyone would come after me, he must deny himself
and take up his cross daily and follow me.*
(Luke 9:23)

A cross wasn't just a symbol of pain and suffering; it
was mainly a symbol of death. Jesus was telling them
they needed to put to death their own plans and desires,
and then turn their lives over to Him and to do His will
every day. He said, *"Anyone who does not carry his
cross and follow me cannot be my disciple"* (Luke
14:27). Is Christ the master of your life? Have you put
to death your own plans and committed yourself to His
will for your life? Don't be satisfied with anything less;
for there is no greater joy in life than following Christ
every day. Billy Graham    www.BillyGraham.org
© 2019 Billy Graham Evangelistic Association

# Table of Contents

# Foreword

It is a pleasure to recommend the careful reading of this book: *Salvation of the Soul*. In it, we finally have a straightforward, easy to read, and an understandable presentation of sanctification.

James Harman traces through scripture that which is meant by *spirit salvation* and *soul salvation*...confusion greatly abounds by generally being taught as one and the same. Sadly, there is great failure in the church today, in not separating and teaching the meanings of soul and spirit (Heb 4:12).

Mr. Harman carefully presents the identification of each in conjunction with salvation. He shows us how that upon believing in the Lord Jesus Christ for the payment of our sins, for which He gave His life on the cross, we receive the GIFT (without merit or works) of eternal life: *spirit salvation*.

He shows us how as believers, we are thereafter exhorted with the necessity of "Godly living" (workmanship) if we are to experience *soul salvation* as a reward (not a gift).

As you read, you will discover that *spirit salvation* and *soul salvation* will also include the final salvation in the resurrection of the body: the rapture (I Thess 4:13-17; I Cor 15:54).

Mr. Harman discloses the vital aspects of the salvation of the soul required to qualify for positions of responsibility to "rule and reign" in the millennial Kingdom of 1,000 years. These are obtained... *"if so be"* (Rom 8:17) that we present our bodies as living sacrifices to the Lord Jesus Christ...to do His will.

Additionally, he shows us that the sanctified believer, "the overcomer," and the one receiving the "salvation of the soul" are all the same. Having lived for Christ, obeyed the Lord and presented his natural life as a living sacrifice…this believer will have an abundant entrance into the millennial Kingdom of Christ.

Knowing this, let us diligently *"press on to the prize of the high calling of God in Christ Jesus"* (Phil 3:14).

Lewis Schoettle, Ed. D.
Schoettle Publishing Company
www.SchoettlePublishing.com

# Introduction

We are about to explore a teaching that has received very little attention by today's Church. The distinction between the salvation of the spirit and the salvation of the soul is of vital importance to the future destiny of every believer.

I am only aware of a handful of authors who have written books on the subject of the salvation of the soul. While there are several expositors who deal quite admirably with the subject, there is a great need in the body of Christ to properly understand the immense consequences of "rightly dividing" this topic.

Most believers equate being "born again" the same as "saving their soul." As we will discover in this brief study, being born again is really only the first step. A person is born again when they realize their need for a Saviour and acknowledge Jesus Christ as their own personal Saviour, as described in the Prologue and the Special Invitation at the back of this book.

If the reader has never responded to Christ before, please take the time to do so now before proceeding. This entire study is designed for all of those who have been born from above.

Once a person is born again, the Holy Spirit comes to reside in the believer. This facet is illustrated in the diagram found on the next page. The person's spirit is saved and guaranteed to be with God for eternity. This is based on the finished work of Christ on the cross, and the person's spirit is justified before God forever. The salvation of the believer's spirit is secure and can never be lost again.

*In Him you also trusted, after you heard the word of truth, the gospel of your salvation; in whom also, having believed, you were **sealed with** the Holy Spirit of promise.* (Eph 1:13)

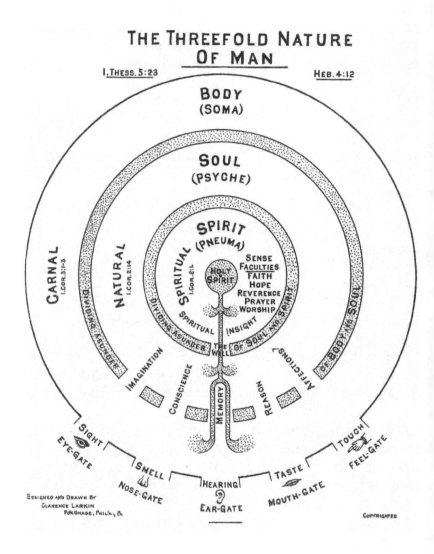

The above picture is from **Dispensational Truth,** by Clarence Larkin, page 99, © 1918. Used with permission of the Rev. Clarence Larkin Estate, P.O. Box 334, Glenside, PA 19038, U.S.A., 215-576-5590, www.larkinestate.com

Man was created in the image of God who is triune: God the Father, God the Son and God the Holy Spirit. Man likewise consists of three parts: body, soul and spirit.

The spirit of man is *"the lamp of the Lord, searching all the innermost parts of his being"* (Pro 20:27 – NASB). The spirit of man connects us with God, who searches out our hearts. But Adam's sin in the garden of Eden brought death to everybody:

*When Adam sinned, sin entered the world. Adam's sin brought death, so death spread to everyone, for everyone sinned.*
(Rom 5:12 – NLT)

Spiritual death caused all of mankind to be separated from God. To remedy the situation, God sent His Son to reconcile man back to Himself. <u>Our spirit</u> is saved when we are born again by believing on the Lord Jesus Christ. After a person is saved spiritually, the issue revolves around the salvation of the soul.

When God created man from the dust of the ground, He breathed life into him, and he became a "living soul" (*cf.* Gen 2:7 – KJV). The soul of man is our mind, will and intellect. It refers to our <u>natural life</u>, which is the seat of our desires, our emotions and personality. Our soul is who we are as a person.

The salvation of the soul is dependent on the life that we live after our spirit is saved. If we allow the Holy Spirit to control our life we can realize the salvation of our soul. If we allow our <u>carnal nature</u> to dominate, we are in danger of losing our soul when we stand before the Judgment Seat of Christ.

---

*For the word of God is living and powerful, and sharper than any two-edged sword, piercing even to the division of <u>soul and spirit, and of joints and marrow</u>, and is a discerner of the thoughts and intents of the heart.* (Hbr 4:12)

God's original purpose in creating man was to give him dominion over His glorious creation (*cf.* Gen 1:26-28). God's magnificent plan is to restore the world when Jesus Christ returns to reestablish His righteous Kingdom over all the earth. Jesus Christ is seeking out a righteous remnant of believers who will be qualified to rule and reign with Him.

The qualification of every person who has been born again will be determined when we individually stand before Christ at the Judgment Seat. This judgment is for every person who has experienced the salvation of their spirit. The issue to be examined by Jesus revolves around the faithfulness of the believer and whether they have been successful in realizing the salvation of their soul.

The purpose of this book is to help believers examine their lives and assist them in becoming faithful overcomers who will be qualified to rule and reign with Christ in the coming Kingdom. After we have experienced the salvation of our spirit, it is imperative that we allow the Word of God to sanctify us completely in order to realize the salvation of our soul.

*Now may the God of peace Himself sanctify you completely;*
*and may your whole* <u>*spirit, soul, and body*</u> *be preserved*
*blameless at the coming of our Lord Jesus Christ.* (1Th 5:23)

---

*"So somewhere there exists a draft by the hand of God of what our life might have been, and still can be; some have lived wonderfully near God's thought for them: let us find and follow that Divine original."*[2] (D.M. Panton – 1870 to 1955)

# Chapter 1 – Salvation: Past, Present and Future

**Salvation of the Spirit – Past Aspect: I have been saved**
As we begin to look into such a great salvation spoken of in the book of Hebrews, it is important to remember that our salvation is provided by the Lord Jesus Christ, *"for there is none other name under heaven given among men, whereby we must be saved."* (Act 4:12 – KJV)

The salvation that is made available to all mankind is provided by the finished work of Christ when He was crucified for our sins at Calvary. As John Newton's renowned song so wonderfully declares:

> *"Amazing grace! How sweet the sound,*
> *That saved a wretch like me!*
> *I once was lost, but now am found;*
> *Was blind, but now I see."*

Yes, the salvation given to us is based entirely upon the amazing grace of God. All facets of our salvation (past, present and future) are because of God's marvelous grace. Because of His abounding mercy, He freely bestows salvation to all who believe on His name. The salvation of the spirit, which occurs when we are born again, is fully due to the grace of God:

> *8) For by **grace** you have been saved through **faith**,*
> *and that not of yourselves; it is the gift of God,*
> *9) not of works, lest anyone should boast.* (Eph 2:8-9)

The apostle Paul's letter to the Ephesians declares that our salvation is exclusively the work of God and not the work of man. This passage clearly demonstrates the past aspect of our spiritual rebirth by stating: *"you have been saved,"* which shows it is something that was accomplished in the past. Our spiritual rebirth took place the moment we believed on Jesus to save us. It is the present possession of every believer, and it is based entirely on the grace of God. It is eternally secure, having been sealed with the Holy Spirit, who entered into our spirit, establishing an entirely new creation:

> *Therefore if anyone is in Christ [that is, grafted in, joined to Him by faith in Him as Savior], he is a new creature [reborn and renewed by the Holy Spirit]; the old things [<u>the previous moral and spiritual condition</u>] have passed away. Behold, new things have come [because spiritual awakening brings a new life].* (2Cr 5:17 – AMP)

### Justification by Faith

Every person who is born into this world inherits Adam's fallen nature. In other words, we are born into this life with a spirit that is separated and alienated from God (*cf.* Eph 2:12; Col 1:21). When we are *born again*, we become a brand new person who is able to reconnect with our Creator. This marvelous awakening restores our spirit to what God originally intended. This <u>salvation of the spirit</u> is a gift from God we receive by faith. This is known by the doctrine of **justification by faith**.

> *For all have sinned and fall short of the glory of God, **being justified freely** by His grace through the redemption that is in Christ Jesus.* (Rom 3:23-24)

The salvation of the spirit occurs by faith in the finished work of Jesus Christ in redeeming or justifying us before God. This salvation is a work of God by His magnificent grace. Man did not do anything to earn it, and there is nothing man can do to lose it because it is a gift of God.

> *That which is born of the flesh is flesh, and that which is born of Spirit is spirit.* (Jhn 3:6)

> At this point the reader should be certain that they have experienced the salvation of their spirit. Please take a moment to review the **Special Invitation** at the back of this book to ensure you have acknowledged Jesus Christ as your personal Saviour. It is vital that your spirit has been *"born of the Spirit"* before you continue in this study.

**Salvation of the Soul – Present Aspect: I am being saved**
After a person experiences the salvation of their spirit and the Holy Spirit comes to reside within, a battle begins for the person's soul. The soul is our natural life, which we express through our mind, our will and our emotions. The word for soul in the Greek is *psyche* (G 5590), and it is the seat of our feelings, desires, and affections. The natural inclinations of the soul are not automatically aligned with the desires of the new righteous spirit. In other words, the soul wants to gratify the old sinful nature, while the spirit is now led by the Holy Spirit.

*For those who are living according to the flesh set their minds on the things of the flesh [which gratify the body], but those who are living according to the Spirit, [set their minds on] the things of the Spirit [His will and purpose].* (Rom 8:5 – AMP)

The conflict between the soul and the spirit exists in every person who has been born again. It began the moment we were saved and it will continue until we die or we are raptured by the Lord. The Holy Spirit wants our soul to be saved; however, our old flesh nature wants to gratify itself with all the worldly pleasures of this life.

The salvation of the soul represents an ongoing present struggle that will continue for as long as we live:

*Receiving the <u>end of your faith</u>—*
*the **salvation of your souls**. (1Pe 1:9)*

While the **salvation of the spirit** occurred in the past when we were born again, the salvation of the soul will not be realized until the end of our faith. The **salvation of the soul** will not be achieved until we stand before Christ at the Judgment Seat. It represents a continuing work of God in our life that requires our cooperation: *"...work out your own salvation with fear and trembling; for it is God who works in you both to will and to do for His good pleasure"* (Phl 2:12-13).

The apostle Paul is warning us that we need to allow God to help us work out our salvation with **fear** and **trembling** in order for us to obtain the salvation of our soul. This admonition by Paul is extremely important because our Lord taught that it is possible for the believer to lose their soul. The loss of the soul does NOT mean the believer loses their salvation because the believer's spiritual salvation is guaranteed and can NEVER be lost. Every believer's name is written in the Lamb's Book of Life (*cf.* Rev 21:27), and their spiritual salvation is eternally secure – all believers will be with the Lord throughout eternity.

As we shall see later in this study, the loss of the soul has to do with rewards in the coming Kingdom, but not all believers will receive rewards at the Judgment Seat of Christ.

### Sanctification

We have seen that in the **salvation of the spirit** we are justified before God by our faith in Jesus Christ and we can say: "I have been saved." The process related to the **salvation of the soul** is known as sanctification, which requires our cooperation with the desires of the Holy Spirit.

*Now may the God of peace Himself **sanctify you completely**; and may your whole spirit, soul, and body be preserved **blameless** at the coming of our Lord Jesus Christ.* (1Th 5:23)

God's desire is for all believers to be  completely  sanctified  in our entire being: **spirit, soul and body**. Our spirit is sanctified when we are born again and the Holy Spirit takes up permanent residence in our life. The sanctification of our soul requires our daily walk with the Lord as we allow Him to mold us into the person that He wants us to be. Oswald Chambers described the cost of sanctification as follows:

> The reason some of us have not entered into the experience of sanctification is that we have not realized the meaning of sanctification from God's perspective. Sanctification means being made one with Jesus so that the nature that controlled Him will control us. Are we really prepared for what that will cost? It will cost absolutely everything in us which is not of God.[1]

The salvation of the soul involves our collaboration with the Holy Spirit as we allow Him to finish the work God designed for us so that we can be presented blameless *at the coming of our Lord Jesus Christ* (i.e., the Judgment Seat of Christ).

Once we have been born again, we should enter on a journey of becoming more and more like Jesus every day. The salvation of the soul is an ongoing process in which we can say: "I am being saved." The sanctification of our soul is so very important that the Lord took the time to pray the following prayer for us and His disciples just prior to His crucifixion:

*17) Sanctify them by Your truth. Your word is truth…*
*"19) And for their sakes I sanctify Myself,*
*that they also may be sanctified by the truth.* (Jhn 17:17, 19)

---

Some readers may have never learned about sanctification and the salvation of the soul. The remaining chapters of this book are designed to help you discover how the Word of God can facilitate you on this most essential undertaking.

---

**Salvation of the Body – Future Aspect: I will be saved**
As our bodies grow old they continue in a state of deterioration, which will eventually lead to death: *"... Who will deliver me from this body of death?"* (Rom 7:24) But when Jesus died for our sins, He paid for the redemption of our entire being, which included our mortal bodies:

> *Even we ourselves groan within ourselves, eagerly waiting for the adoption, the* **redemption of our body**. (Rom 8:23)

Of course the redemption of our bodies is a future event in which all believers are able to say: "I will be saved."

Since God is a tripartite being (*cf.* Gen 1:26) and man was made in the image of God, we also consist of the three aspects described earlier: **spirit, soul** and **body**. God's design is to see the complete salvation of all three aspects of our being.

**THE THREE ASPECTS OF OUR SALVATION**

| Spirit | Soul | Body |
|---|---|---|
| Past Event | Present/Ongoing | Future Event |
| *I have been saved* | *I am being saved* | *I will be saved* |
| Justification | Sanctification | Redemption |

Once we acknowledge Jesus Christ as our personal Saviour the Holy Spirit comes to dwell in our being. We become a new creation that is justified to live with God throughout eternity. Our spiritual salvation is based on the finished work of Jesus Christ at Calvary, and it is forever sealed by the Holy Spirit (*cf.* Eph 1:13). The salvation of our spirit is 100 percent guaranteed.

The remainder of this book will explain how you can realize the salvation of your soul when you stand before Jesus. For those who approach the rest of this study with a humble and contrite spirit (Isa 66:2), be assured: *"He who has begun a good work in you will complete it until the day of Jesus Christ"* (Phl 1:6).

# Chapter 2 – Cost of Sanctification

—————————◇◆◇—————————

*Then said Jesus **unto his disciples**,*
*If any man will come after me, let him deny himself,*
*and take up his cross, and follow me.* (Mat 16:24 – KJV)

In the passage found in Matthew 16, Jesus had taken His disciples aside in the region of Caesarea Philippi to tell them various matters to come. His teaching on the salvation of the soul is found in verses 24–27, and has been the source of a great deal of confusion in the Church today. Eminent lawyer Philip Mauro, who wrote the brief that Bryan used in the famous Tennessee-Scopes trial in 1925, also advocated upholding sound doctrine in Christianity. Regarding this subject he noted:

> The subject of the salvation of the soul has not been satisfactorily treated in any of the books of teaching in the hands of the people of God….Being "born again," and "saving the soul," are generally taken to be identical. But according to the Scripture, the two are very different. The salvation of the soul is distinctly referred to as something *future*, and as something *conditional upon the behavior of the individual himself.* In the words of the Lord Himself, not as a gift, but as a ***reward*** to be earned by diligence, stead-fastness and obedience to His commands.[1]

While Mauro's astute observations were made over one hundred years ago, not much has really changed. The teaching on the salvation of the soul is regrettably lacking in today's Church. To make matters even worse, many erroneously believe that Christ's teaching in Matthew 16 is to the unsaved!

**If Any Disciple**
In context, Jesus was saying: *"If any of you wants to be my follower…"* (Mat 16:24 – NLT). In other words, the instructions

Jesus was about to give were directed at those who want to be devoted pupils of His teachings. The entire purpose of the principles He was about to give was for their own edification. The instructions on the *salvation of the soul* are for believers who want to be His disciples.

**Denying Oneself**
The first directive Jesus gives involves giving control of our lives over to the direction of the Holy Spirit. Denying oneself means dying to self and allowing God to take over. This goes against our natural inclinations and is impossible to accomplish in our own strength.

Our carnal bodies are in a war with our new redeemed spirit for our soul. The Spirit wants to save the soul, but the flesh wants to gratify and please itself. If our old flesh nature wins the battle, our soul is lost. But through the power of the Holy Spirit, we can overcome the old fleshly nature of our soul and keep our bodies under subjection.

*13) For if you <u>live according to the flesh you will die</u>; but if by the Spirit you **put to death** the deeds of the body, **you will live**. 14) For as many as are led by the Spirit of God, these are sons of God. (Rom 8:13-14)*

Denying oneself requires making a decision every day of our life to allow the Holy Spirit to rule and reign over us.

Denying oneself requires a balancing act because we all have personal needs: food, clothing, shelter, etc. The problem arises when things, we **think** we need, become **indulgences**. God's desire is for all our needs to be met (Phl 4:19), but everything should be done in moderation and not out of lust for things:

*15) Do not love the world or the things in the world. If anyone loves the world, the love of the Father is not in him.*

*16) For all that is in the world—the lust of the flesh,*
*the lust of the eyes, and the pride of life—*
*is not of the Father but is of the world.* (1Jo 2:15-16)

The key to winning the battle is allowing the Holy Spirit to help us from indulging in and loving the things of this world – for the world and all its lusts are passing away.

The struggle is amplified for today's Christians living in modern America. Our nation is the leading importer of goods that supply the profuse flow of merchandise to satisfy the desires of a country with less than 5 percent of the world's population. The cry by the voice from heaven to "**come out of her, my people**" (Rev 18:4) is an admonition believers need to pay attention to so we don't end up thinking that all of our many "wants" really represent our true needs.

## Take Up One's Cross

The second instruction Jesus gives for us to be His disciple is somewhat related to the first one since "*taking up one's cross*" also involves death. The cross was the instrument used in the crucifixion and Jesus is telling us that we need to be willing to take up whatever cross God may bring into our life. Luke's account shows that this also requires a *daily* commitment:

*If any one doth will to come after me, let him disown himself,*
*and take up his cross daily, and follow me;*
(Luk 9:23 – YLT)

It is important to understand that a "cross" is not something that we bring upon ourselves, which could come about because of bad choices or anything resulting from our own sins. The "cross" Jesus is describing is some kind of suffering that God allows to come our way. The varieties are endless, including such things as severe health issues, major financial setbacks, family heartaches, religious persecution, and the list goes on....

Jesus is saying that we need to be willing to respond properly to whatever difficulty God may allow in our life. God has a purpose in allowing trials of various kinds to come our way, which we will learn more about in the following chapter.

### Profit and Exchange – Reward and Works

*25) For whosoever will **save his life** (i.e., <u>soul</u>) **shall lose it**: and whosoever will **lose his life** (i.e., <u>soul</u>) for my sake shall find it. 26) For what is a man **profited**, if he shall **gain the whole world**, and **lose his own** <u>soul</u>? or what shall a man give in **exchange** for his <u>soul</u>?*

> *27) For the Son of man shall come in the glory of his Father with his angels; and <u>then</u> he shall **reward** every man according to his **works**.* (Mat 16:25-27 – KJV)

After Jesus tells us we are required to 1) deny self, 2) take up our cross, and 3) follow Him, He then gives an analogy of how we can **save our soul**, which can be illustrated as follows:

| Save Soul Now | Lose Soul Now |
|---|---|
| Lose Soul at the Judgment Seat of Christ | Save Soul at the Judgment Seat of Christ |

If we are <u>not willing</u> to deny ourselves, take up our cross, and follow Christ in our current life (<u>indulge our soul now</u>), we will **lose our soul** when Jesus comes and forfeit our rewards.

If we are <u>willing</u> to deny ourselves, take up our cross and follow Christ in our current life (<u>lose our soul now</u>) we will be able to **save our soul** when Jesus comes and receive great rewards.

From verse 27, we can see that when Jesus returns at His second coming, He will **reward** us according to our **works**, i.e., by whether we have been faithful disciples. The <u>salvation of our spirit</u> is based upon our *Past Salvation*, while the <u>salvation of our soul</u> is based upon our *Present/Ongoing Salvation*.

### THE TWO ASPECTS OF SALVATION

| Past Aspect of Our Salvation | | |
|---|---|---|
| **Salvation of the Spirit** | **Justification by Faith** | **Free Gift** **Heaven** |

| Present/Ongoing Aspect of Our Salvation | | |
|---|---|---|
| **Salvation of the Soul** | **Justification by Works** | **Reward** **Kingdom** |

Jesus is teaching that if we want to be His disciples we must perform certain **works** (deny self, take up our cross and follow Him) if we are to **save our soul**. If we are successful, He will **reward** us when we stand before the Judgment Seat. This **justification by works**[2] was also alluded to by the apostle Paul:

> 8) For <u>by grace</u> you have been saved <u>through faith</u>,
> and that not of yourselves; it is the <u>gift of God</u>,
> 9) <u>not of works</u>, lest anyone should boast
> 10) For we are His workmanship, <u>created</u> in Christ Jesus
> <u>for good works</u>, which God prepared [ordained – KJV]
> beforehand that <u>we should walk in them</u>. (Eph 2:8-10)

The *salvation of our spirit* is completely by the grace of God. We are justified by our faith in Jesus, and we are guaranteed to reside with the Lord forever. Our spirit was sanctified because Christ willingly gave up His life and died for us (crucifixion).

We were saved by faith to do the good works which God prepared for us to do. The *salvation of our soul* depends upon our surrendering control of our life to the Holy Spirit. When we live our life under the control and the power of the Holy Spirit, we will realize the sanctification of our soul and produce the good works God planned for us. This will result in rewards and a position of honor in the coming Kingdom when Jesus returns.

Sanctification of our soul requires **giving up our life for Him**.

New believers and those who are unfamiliar with the topic
on the _salvation of the soul_ may want to review Appendix 1,
which describes the subject entitled: **_The Crucified Life_**.
Readers are encouraged to read the information in the
appendixes as you continue this brief study.

## Summary

Every person who has been born again received the free gift of
eternal life. The _salvation of our spirit_ has been sealed by the
Holy Spirit, and we are guaranteed to reside with the Lord
throughout eternity. Jesus taught on the _salvation of the soul_
because He wants us to be able to realize rewards when our life
is complete and we stand before the Judgment Seat.

In the following chapter we will learn how James, the half
brother of our Lord Jesus Christ, also taught on the _salvation of
the soul_ because this teaching can produce great rewards in our
lives.

# Chapter 3 – Receive the Implanted Word

The book of James is misunderstood by many in the Church today and some have even questioned whether it should be included in the Bible. In the following chapter we will learn why Martin Luther rejected the book as part of Scripture. And yet, this epistle is an integral ingredient in understanding the important subject on the *salvation of the soul*.

James wrote one of the first books of the New Testament during a time when the early Christians were experiencing tremendous persecution. Not surprisingly, he begins by saying:

*2) My brethren, **count it all joy** when you fall into various <u>trials</u>, 3) knowing that the <u>testing</u> of your faith produces **patience**.*[5281] *4) But let **patience** have its perfect work, that you may be **perfect**[5046] and **complete**, lacking nothing. (Jam 1:2-4)*

Numerous believers assume that when they are born again life will be a *bed of roses* and their new life in Christ will be without a lot of problems or concerns. Christians who read their Bibles know this is not necessarily the case, and many can probably quote the above verses to help those who are going through difficulties.

## Enduring Trials: James 1:2-12

Contrary to our natural inclinations, James is teaching us that we should be happy and joyful when God allows troubles to come our way. This attitude sounds like foolishness to those who don't know Christ; however, our Lord dearly loves every believer, and He holds each one of us in His hands.

The reason trials are permitted in our lives is to allow our faith to grow. James tells us that the testing of our faith is to produce patience. The Greek word for *patience* is *hypomonē* (G 5281), and it stands for endurance and perseverance. The purpose God has in allowing trials is for our faith to develop into maturity by learning to persevere. His desire is for us to be perfect and complete. The Greek word for *perfect* is *teleios* (G 5046), which means brought to its end, wanting nothing, perfect, full grown, and mature. God permits sufferings and trials in order for us to become mature believers.

Significantly, *teleios* is the same word that our Lord used in the Sermon on the Mount: *"Therefore you shall be perfect,*[5046]*just as your Father in heaven is perfect"* (Mat 5:48).

Both Jesus and James's desire is for believers to become mature in our faith so we can be considered true overcomers. Learning to be an overcomer is perhaps the most difficult thing to do on this earth as a human being. The overcomer is born through the victory we receive by trusting in Jesus Christ. Though we may be thrown into the furnace of affliction, we can come forth as pure gold if we love the Lord and trust Him to see us through.

Relating to trials, Matthew Henry commented: "The believer needs not fear the fiery trial of afflictions and temptations, by which the Saviour refines his gold. He will take care it is not more intense or longer than is needful for his good"[1]

And the apostle Peter's explanation of why God allows us to go through various trials is very similar to those advanced by James:

*7) That the **trial of your faith**, being much **more precious than of gold** that perisheth, though it be tried with fire, might be found unto praise and honour and glory at the appearing of Jesus Christ: 8) **Whom having not seen, ye love**; in whom, though now ye see him not, yet believing, ye **rejoice with joy unspeakable** and full of glory:* (1Pe 1:7-8 – KJV)

God permits trials to come our way because He wants us to become mature believers who love Him. Those who pass the test will be richly rewarded when Jesus Christ returns to reward those who are found faithful. The reward that He promises to give to those who love Him is the *"crown of life."*

*Blessed* is the one who *perseveres* under *trial* because, having stood the test, that person will *receive* the *crown of life* that the Lord has *promised to those who love him.* (Jam 1:12 – NIV)

Standing before Jesus at the Judgment Seat can be our most glorious moment when He will richly reward us for our perseverance. What a magnificent day is in store for the overcomers.

*Weeping may endure for a night,*
*But joy comes in the morning.* (Psa 30:5)

## Resisting Temptations: James 1:13-21

*13) Let no one say when he is tempted, 'I am being tempted by God'; for God cannot be tempted by evil, and He Himself does not tempt anyone. 14) But each one is tempted when he is carried away and enticed by his own lust.*
(Jam 1:13-14 – NASB)

In addition to the various trials, which God allows into our lives to teach us how we can rely upon His strength to overcome and become mature believers, we are also tempted by our own lusts.

When we were born again we received a new nature that is born of God (*cf.* 1Jo 3:9). While this "new man" does not sin, we still have our old flesh nature. Our carnal flesh can tempt us, and we can be *"carried away"* to sin. If we allow the "old man" within us to give in to our lusts, James tells us: *"And sin, when it is full-grown, brings forth death"* (Jam 1:15).

Here, James is speaking of the death of our **soul** – remember, the **spirit's** salvation is completely secure. He is warning us not to allow our old flesh nature to entice us to sin. When tempted, we must immediately rebuke it and call upon the Lord to give us the power to resist it.

After warning about the dangers of giving in to our carnal nature, he continues by providing the key ingredient to victory over sin:

> *For the wrath[3709] of man does not produce*
> *the righteousness of God.* (Jam 1:20)

The Greek word for *wrath* (G 3709) is *orgē*, which means the natural disposition, impulse or desire. As noted by Mize: "The equivalent English word, which comes from the Latin, is *libido*. Libido has come to mean sexual desire just as *orgē* has come to mean anger, but the first definition is much broader in scope, meaning all basic desires for pleasure. It is the desires of the flesh nature or the lust of the flesh described in James 1:14. With the above understanding of the meaning of *orgē*, this verse could be accurately paraphrased as follows:

> *For the natural desires of man's sin nature does not bring*
> *about that which is righteous in God's sight"*
> (Jam 1:20 Paraphrase)."[2]

> *Therefore lay aside all filthiness and overflow of wickedness,*
> *and **receive with meekness the implanted word**,*
> *which is able to **save your souls**.* (Jam 1:21)

James used the words *"filthiness and overflow of wickedness"* to refer back to *orgē* in the previous verse. James is telling us that because the natural desires of man's sin nature do not bring about that which is righteous in God's eyes, the Christian needs to get rid of all moral depravity and super-abounding evil. In other words, put away all the sins of our old depraved nature.

After we have resolved in our heart to rid our lives of sin, we are ready to receive that which is able to save our souls. The vital ingredient is to meekly receive the Word, which is engrafted, or implanted, within us. James likens this process to allowing the Word of God to be like a living plant that grows inside of us, empowering the Holy Spirit to bring forth fruit in our lives.

In order to realize the salvation of our souls, we will want to read and study our Bibles with humble and teachable hearts. By asking the Holy Spirit to renew our minds, He will show us how to apply what we learn and bring forth a bountiful harvest in our lives: *"22) But the fruit of the Spirit is love, joy, peace, patience, kindness, goodness, faithfulness, 23) gentleness, self-control"* (Gal 5:22-23 – ESV). The implanted Word will allow us to grow into mature Christians.

### Doers Will Be Blessed: James 1:22-25
> *22) But be **doers of the word,** and **not hearers only,** deceiving yourselves...25) But the one who looks into the perfect law, the law of liberty, **and perseveres,** being no hearer who forgets **but a doer who acts,** he will be **blessed in his doing.** (Jam 1:22, 25 – ESV)*

Many believers come to the Lord and experience the salvation of their spirit; however, they continue allowing their old flesh nature to rule their lives. These same Christians probably do not read the Bible and are considered *"hearers only."* Although they will ultimately go to heaven, they will be missing out on the blessings God has in store for the faithful *doers of the word*.

James is declaring that if we will diligently persevere by allowing the Word of God to shape our lives, we will be blessed. The blessing he is referring to is the salvation of our souls, which will result in being rewarded with the crown of life as he described earlier.

The apostle Paul also taught on the salvation of our soul in a similar manner:

*1) I beseech you therefore, brethren, by the mercies of God, that you **present your bodies a living sacrifice, holy, acceptable** to God, which is your reasonable service. 2) And **do not be conformed to this world**, but be **transformed by the renewing of your mind**, that you may prove what is that good and acceptable and perfect will of God.* (Rom 12:1-2)

*22) **Put off your old self**, which belongs to your former manner of life and is corrupt through deceitful desires, 23) and to **be renewed in the spirit of your minds**,* (Eph 4:22-23 – ESV)

Paul exhorts believers not to live like the world does or like we used to live before we were Christians. Like James, we are to "put off" or "cast away" the things of our old flesh nature and to be inwardly transformed by the renewing of our minds.

Magnificent rewards are in store for believers who persevere under trial, resist temptations and permit the Word of God to empower us to live fruitful, victorious lives by the renewing of our minds.

When we stand in front of Jesus at the Judgment Seat, we will be so very glad that we persevered! All our trials, tests, heartaches and sorrows will be over. The joy of seeing Christ's approving smile will be worth it all!

---

New believers and those who are unfamiliar with the topic of being an *overcomer* may want to review Appendix 2 at this point. Overcomers are those mature Christians who will realize the salvation of their soul when they stand before the Judgment Seat of Christ and experience unspeakable joy!

# Chapter 4 – Faithful to God's Calling

*14) What does it **profit**, <u>my brethren</u>, if someone says he has faith but does not have works? Can faith **save him**?*
*20) But do you want to know, O foolish man, that faith without works is dead? [fn] 21) Was not Abraham our father **justified by works** when he offered Isaac his son on the altar?*
(Jam 2:14, 20-21)    [fn] NU-Text reads useless

The second chapter of James has been the source of a great deal of confusion in understanding how a person is saved. All the perplexity goes away when we understand the context of what James is speaking of and the aspect of salvation he is addressing.

First of all, notice that James is talking with his brothers and sisters in Christ. The context is to believers, and his rhetorical questions have to do with their salvation, not the unconverted.

The judgment for believers is the Judgment Seat of Christ, and this is what the above passage of Scripture is dealing with. All Christians will appear before this judgment, and their spiritual salvation is not under consideration. They have already been justified by grace due to their faith in Jesus Christ.

In the previous chapter James introduced the central message of his book: the salvation of the soul. He continues this teaching by asking how a person's works relate to their salvation.

---

The problem arises when people assume that James is speaking on the salvation of the spirit. If that were the case (and it is not), James would be referring to the Great White Throne Judgment at the end of the millennium. This judgment is for those who have never received Christ as their Saviour; this is not the judgment he was addressing.

---

## Profit and *Salvation of the Soul*

James asked fellow believers two rhetorical questions as to whether their works would realize a profit when they stood before the Judgment Seat and whether such faith would save them. To understand the issues, it may be helpful to paraphrase what James is asking:

> *Brothers and sisters in Christ, if anyone says he is a believer, but he does not have any works to show for his life, he cannot profit, can he? His faith (without any works) cannot save his soul, can it?*

In his example, the person has faith (he is a believer), but he does not have any works. The answer to both questions is obviously no, but let's see what this means.

When a believer stands before Christ without anything to show for his life, he will be like the person in the parable of the talents (Mat 25:14-30) who hid his talent in the ground and did not have any profit to give the Lord when He returned. His faith without any works was unprofitable. In James 2, the word "dead" appears in connection with verses 17, 20, and 26; but Arlen Chitwood noted, "In a number of the older Greek manuscripts the word 'barren' or 'fruitless,' is used in verse 20 instead of the word 'dead'" (Chitwood, p. 74).

James is telling us that a believer who does not provide any works to show for his life has a faith that is barren or unfruitful. This believer is still saved, and he will be in heaven; however, his faith did not provide any profit. His life will not be rewarded when he stands before Christ. In other words, James is saying that a believer without any works has a barren faith and this person will not realize the salvation of his *soul*. His *spirit* is saved and he will be in heaven throughout eternity, but he will greatly regret the fact that he lived his life for himself instead of living his life to please the Lord.

## Justification by Works

The fact that James teaches we are justified by our works has greatly perplexed many Christians. Because we know that the apostle Paul teaches we are justified by grace through faith, this teaching by James appears to be a contradiction. Throughout church history this apparent incongruity has created significant disagreement. Martin Luther went so far to contend that the book of James should not even be included in our canon of Scripture.

This seeming disagreement is resolved when we understand which aspect of salvation is being addressed. Paul's teaching that we are justified by faith relates to the salvation of our spirit.

> *8) For by **grace** you have been saved through **faith**,*
> *and that not of yourselves; it is the gift of God,*
> *9) not of works, lest anyone should boast.* (Eph 2:8-9)

When we come to the cross and believe that Jesus died for our sins, we are born from above by grace through faith. Our *spirit* is reborn by our faith and faith alone – works have absolutely nothing to do with the salvation of our *spirit*.

After we are born again, the apostle Paul also said: *"For we are His workmanship, created in Christ Jesus for good works, which God prepared beforehand that we should walk in them"* (Eph 2:10). Paul is saying we were saved to do the good works God has designed for us. While the *salvation of our spirit* is totally by faith, God wants us to carry out His plan for our life. That plan includes completing His divine purpose.

The central message in the book of James relates to the *salvation of the soul*. We can accomplish this if we persevere under trial, resist temptation, receive the Word of God into our lives and become doers of the Word and not only hearers. We need to remember that the salvation of our *spirit* occurred when we were born again and that the salvation of our *soul* is an ongoing process, which will not be completed until we stand before Jesus. The salvation of our *soul* will be based on whether we have been successful in fulfilling God's plan for us. James is saying that we will be *justified by our works* if we have accomplished those things, which God prepared in advance for us to do...being faithful to His calling.

### Faithful to One's Calling

Since James is telling us that the salvation of our *soul* is to be based on our works, we need to understand what this actually means. He provides the answer by giving us two different and unique examples to help explain that for which God is looking.

### Father of the Faithful

Abraham is known as the father of the faithful and is one of those mentioned in Hebrews 11, known as the great faith chapter, which begins with the definition of faith: *"Now faith is the substance of things hoped for, the evidence of things not seen"* (Heb 11:1). It is important to remember that Abraham was justified by faith and faith <u>alone</u> when the Lord said to him:

> *"5) Look now toward heaven, and count the stars if you are able to number them." And He said to him, "So shall your descendants be." 6) And **he believed in the Lord**, and He accounted it to him for **righteousness**.* (Gen 15:5-6)

Abraham's initial faith corresponds to the believer's initial faith, which is totally by faith (*cf.* Rom 4:2-5, 5:1-2, Eph 2:8-9). We are justified by faith and have peace with God as a free gift. This initial faith is without any works, and we receive the promise of eternal life in the same manner Abraham received the above promise.

After his initial faith, he obeyed God's calling in his life. Following a period of over fifty years living as a pilgrim in a strange land, he and Sarah gave birth to God's promised child. During this time, Abraham's faith was tried, allowing it to mature. God tested him further by asking him to offer up his only son as a sacrifice. James applies Abraham's faithfulness to God's calling in his life to illustrate *justification by works*:

> *21) Was not Abraham our father **justified by works**
> when he offered Isaac his son on the altar?
> 22) Do you see that **faith** was working together with his **works**,
> and by **works faith was made perfect**$^{5048}$?* (Jam 2:21-22)

Because Abraham was obedient to God's calling in His life, his faith had fully matured and it was considered perfect. The Greek word *Teleioō* (G 5048) comes from *teleios* (G 5046), which is the same word the Lord used in the Sermon on the Mount. James is telling us that if our faith is accompanied by works, our faith will be full grown, mature and perfect. By faithfully carrying out the calling God had for his life, Abraham was also considered a friend of God:

> *Abraham believed God, and it was accounted to him for righteousness. And he was **called the friend of God**.* (Jam 2:23)

Being saved does not mean we are automatically called a friend of God (*cf.* Joh 15:14). Abraham earned this title because he was obedient and faithful to the calling God had on his life. After we are saved, we should likewise be faithful in carrying out the calling God has for our life.

### Rahab the Harlot
> ***Likewise**, was not Rahab the harlot also **justified by works**
> when she received the messengers
> and sent them out another way?* (Jam 2:25)

The second example that James uses to show justification by works is the harlot Rahab. James says Rahab was likewise or equally justified by her works because she acted by faith to the calling God had for her life: *"by faith Rahab the harlot did not perish with those who disbelieved, having received the spies with peace"* (Heb 11:31 – YLT). Rahab believed God had given the land where she lived to the children of Israel. Because of her faith, she hid the spies Joshua had sent and helped them escape from Jericho. God had called this prostitute to an important task, and she was faithful to her calling! Because of her faithfulness, she was justified by works.

Both Abraham and Rahab acted by faith to the calling that God had for their lives. Because of their faithfulness, they were both equally justified by their works. Every believer falls somewhere between the father of the faithful and that of a lowly prostitute. God wants you to be faithful to the calling He has for you.

**Faithful to God's Calling**
God has a purpose for every person and a calling for every individual He created. His desire is for us to develop a mature faith, and that we will be faithful to the calling He has for us.

God does not need us to do good works for us to get into heaven. Jesus already made the way by faith. God wants us to do good works so that we will realize His calling for our life.

Discover what your calling is and carry out the good works, which God has prepared for you to do (Eph 2:10). For those who are faithful to God's calling, He will bestow upon you eternal rewards, as we will discover in the next chapter.

> Think what would have happened if Abraham and Rahab had not been faithful to their calling. The world as we know it today may be a totally different place. Don't let this happen with your life. God wants you to carry out His master plan for your life – be faithful to His calling for you!

# Chapter 5 – Goal of Our Faith

*22) But you have come to* **Mount Zion** *and to the city of the living God, the* **heavenly Jerusalem***, to an innumerable company of angels, 23) to the general assembly and church of the firstborn who are registered in heaven, to God the Judge of all, to the spirits of just men made* **perfect**[5048](Heb 12:22-23).

New believers and those who are not familiar with some of the meat doctrines (Heb 5:14) in the Word of God, may have been wondering what the Holy City (on the front cover), represents. The book of Hebrews was written to teach believers about the great salvation (Heb 2:3), which we must not ignore or neglect dealing with the salvation of the *soul* and our inheritance in this Holy City. James Hollandsworth noted in *The End of the Pilgrimage*:

> The salvation mentioned in Hebrews is not soteriological,[1] referring to justification. It is referring to the sanctification aspect of salvation, or soul-salvation. Thus, the book is written to believers and focuses on persevering unto reward. At least five warnings are given, urging saints to persevere in their walk with the Lord, or else they could forfeit their inheritance (Hollandsworth, p. 86).

**Inheritance in Jeopardy**

Many in the church today may not be aware of the possible danger that exists regarding our future inheritance.

> *23) And whatever you do, do it heartily, as to the Lord and not to men, 24) knowing that from the Lord you will receive the* **reward of the inheritance***; for you serve the Lord Christ. 25) But he who does wrong will be repaid for what he has done, and there is no partiality.*
> (Col 3:23-25)

The reward of the inheritance, which the apostle Paul is describing in the above passage, is dependent on faithfulness. The just recompense of reward is based on our trustworthy performance. This principle had its roots in the Old Testament with two classic examples where firstborn sons forfeited their inheritance.

Standing in the position as a firstborn son did not by itself guarantee the inheritance. The story of Esau can be found in Genesis 25:27-34. Esau lost his inheritance because he thought very little of it. Esau despised his birthright and sold it for a bowl of stew. Like Esau, Reuben also lost his inheritance. Genesis 35:22, records where he dishonored and shamed his father by sensual pleasure with his father's concubine.

Despite being firstborn sons, both Esau and Reuben lost their inheritance because of disobedience and unfaithfulness. Even though they were in the positions as firstborn, they forfeited the blessings their inheritance could have provided because they were not faithful to their calling.

### Israel in the Wilderness
Similarly, Christians have been given a future inheritance, which may also be in jeopardy, as shown by the analogy of the Israelites leaving Egypt. Israel had been redeemed by God; however, all except Caleb and Joshua were overthrown in the wilderness (*cf.* 1Co 10:1-12, Num 13 &14).

*Now all these things happened to them **as examples**, and they*
*were written for **our admonition**,*
*upon whom the **ends of the ages** have come.* (1Co 10:11)

Caleb and Joshua were the only spies who came back and advised Moses to take possession of the land of Canaan. Because of their faithfulness and obedience to God's Word, they were rewarded with their earthly inheritance. Christians are presently on a pilgrimage journey with a heavenly inheritance in view. The land of Canaan corresponds to inheriting the promise of rest for the people of God (*cf.* Heb 4:9). "So the Rest is the Millennial Reign. For it is the *sabbath* rest, or *seventh millennium*, following on six thousand years of redemption toil...Thus Canaan is the type of the Millennial Kingdom of Christ" (Panton, p. 40). Psalm 95 tells how the Exodus generation failed to enter the land of Canaan:

> *Today, if you will hear His voice: "Do not harden your hearts,*
> *as in the rebellion, As in the day of trial in the wilderness,*
> *When your fathers tested Me;*
> *They tried Me, though they saw My work.*
> *For forty years I was grieved with that generation,*
> *And said, 'It is a people who go astray in their hearts,*
> *And they do not know My ways.'*
> *So I swore in My wrath,*
> *'They shall not enter My rest.'*
> (Psa 95:7-11)

The lesson from the Exodus generation is clear. They failed to enter the land because of disobedience and unfaithfulness. This is a somber warning that should motivate us to remain faithful to the calling God has for us so we may receive the reward of our inheritance. If we are disobedient and unfaithful, we may lose our inheritance in the coming Kingdom of Christ.

Erwin Lutzer begins his book, *Your Eternal Reward* with the first chapter entitled: **"Tears in Heaven,"** by stating: "The judgement seat of Christ is, to our shame, almost universally ignored among Christians." He goes on to say, "I agree with A.J. Gordon, who wrote, 'I cannot think of a final divine reckoning which shall assign the same rank in glory, the same degree of joy to a lazy, indolent and unfruitful Christian as to an ardent, devoted, self-denying Christian." (Lutzer, p. 18)

### Millennial Kingdom Prize

*24) Do you not know that in a race all the runners run, but **only one receives the prize? So run that you may obtain it.***
*27) But I discipline my body and keep it under control, lest after preaching to others **I myself should be disqualified**.*
(1Co 9:24, 27 – ESV)

The apostle Paul understood that we are all in a race that requires faithful perseverance. He realized that even he could be disqualified for the reward, and he continually admonished believers to be led by the Spirit of God in order to win the prize of our heavenly calling.[2]

### City of Reward

The goal of our faith is to realize the salvation of our *soul* when we stand before Christ at the Judgment Seat. If we are found faithful, we will receive the reward of our inheritance granting us the privilege of ruling and reigning with Jesus in the Holy City.

> *22) But you have come to **Mount Zion** and to the city of the living God, the **heavenly Jerusalem,** to an innumerable company of angels, 23) to the general assembly and **church of the firstborn** who are registered in heaven, to God the Judge of all, to the spirits of just men made **perfect**[5048]*
> (Heb 12:22-23.)

The Holy City, the New Jerusalem, (*cf.* Rev 21:2, 10, 23) will be the dwelling place for those who have allowed the Word of God to develop a fully matured faith (perfect), along with Jesus for 1,000 years. This Holy City will apparently orbit around planet Earth for the millennium for all earthly inhabitants to see. After the 1,000 years, God will bring this Holy City down to Earth where it will reside for all the ages to come.

G.H. Lang saw this magnificent city as a reward for the faithful:

The heavenly portion is for that limited portion of the saved known to Scripture as "the church of the firstborn ones who are enrolled in heaven" (Heb 12:23). (1) Their calling to this superior dignity is of grace. (2) Their pathway to it is marked by sharing the sufferings of Christ. (3) Their attaining thereto is the reward that grace will give for the sufferings which grace enabled them to bear unto the end. They might have avoided the sufferings, as in fact many, alas do; in which case they would have fallen short of the grace and have forfeited the reward (Lang, p. 381).

All believers will be part of the coming millennial Kingdom; however, not all will participate in ruling and reigning with Christ. Several expositors have used various analogies to help illustrate this.

It is analogous to a person going to the White House with the idea of being the Director of the FBI, but finding out when he arrives that he will be mowing the lawn. There is going to be weeping by many Christians when they arrive in heaven and discover that they are going to be sweeping up gold dust in the streets. (Note: This is a tongue-in-cheek expression that the late Dr. M.R. DeHaan once used).

I liken [it] to being a subject in a medieval kingdom, for example. The king would own and rule a vast territory. His subjects would benefit from living in the village, under the king's protection and bounty, but only those heirs living in the castle would be able to fully participate in reigning and enjoy the beauties and luxuries and opportunities of the king Himself (Hollandsworth, p. 33).

When we stand before Jesus, it can be one of the most glorious moments of our lives. To hear Him say, *"Well done, good and faithful servant...Enter into the joy of your Lord,"* will be the happiest time we can ever imagine. His smiling face will mean

He is pleased with how we allowed Him to rule and reign in our hearts during this earthly pilgrimage. Because of this, He will grant us the incomparable pleasure of ruling and reigning with Him in the eternal glory to which the God of all grace has called us in Christ.

> *10) Wherefore the rather, brethren,* **give diligence** *to make* **your calling and election sure***: for* <u>*if ye do these things*</u>*, ye shall never fall: 11) For so an entrance shall be ministered unto you* **abundantly into the everlasting kingdom** *of our Lord and Saviour Jesus Christ.* (2Pe 1:10-11 – KJV)

To guarantee a vibrant and fruitful faith, Peter encourages us to add the following vital elements:

> *5) But also for this very reason, giving all diligence,* **add to your faith** *virtue, to virtue knowledge, 6) to knowledge self-control, to self-control perseverance, to perseverance godliness, 7) to godliness brotherly kindness, and to brotherly kindness love. 8) For* **if these things are yours** *and* **abound***, you will be neither barren nor unfruitful in the knowledge of our Lord Jesus Christ.* (2Pe 1:5-8)

By allowing Christ to live His life in us, we will develop into the mature and complete (perfect) believers that He has called us to become. And by allowing the implanted Word to sanctify us completely, we will realize the goal of our faith, the salvation of our *soul*.

> *The approval of your faith..may be discovered after scrutiny to result in praise and glory and honor at the time of the revelation of Jesus Christ; whom having not seen, you love because of His preciousness...you are to be rejoicing with an inexpressible and glorified joy upon the occasion of your receiving the promised consummation of your faith which is the salvation of your souls.* (1Pe 1:7-9)[3]

# Epilogue

---

The Exodus generation rejected "the manna" that God gave them for sustenance and longingly desired to return to the land of Egypt (*cf.* Num 11-14). Today, many believers neglect the food "the Word" which God has provided for nourishment, and they also love the world and the things of this world.

Abraham *"waited for the city which has foundations, whose builder and maker is God"* (Heb 11:10). We are all strangers and pilgrims on this earth, and we should be looking for the heavenly city, which God is preparing for us (*cf.* Heb 11:13-16). This city of reward is getting ready and will be revealed very soon for those who are seeking it with all their heart.

Almost two years ago, as I sat near the Sea of Galilee, the Lord gave me the word: *"Therefore you shall be perfect, just as your Father in heaven is perfect"* (Mat 5:48). These past two years He has been showing me what this really means. Anything that I do in my own strength will end up being wood, hay and stubble, which will be burned up in the trying fire at the Judgment Seat (1Co 3:12-15). But if I allow Christ to live His life in me, He will create works of gold, silver and precious stones through me, which will be evidenced by a faith that is full grown, mature and complete.

I realize that many will reject this writing and say I am teaching a works-based salvation. Ironically, these naysayers will be totally correct. Those who have ears to hear what the Spirit is saying will readily discern that the *salvation of the soul* may be one of the most important teachings in the Bible. These same people will one day hear our Saviour tell them these most wonderful and marvelous words: *Well done!*

*2) Then I, John, saw the **holy city**, New Jerusalem,
coming down out of heaven from God, prepared as a
bride adorned for her husband.10)And he carried me
away in the Spirit...and showed me the great city, the
holy Jerusalem descending out of heaven from God.
23)The city had no need of the sun or the moon to shine
in it, for the glory of God illuminated it.*
*The Lamb is its light.*
(Rev 21:2,10, 23)

---

The Holy City, the New Jerusalem, will be the dwelling
place of Jesus, along with the called, and chosen, and
faithful for 1,000 years. This Holy City will apparently
orbit around planet Earth for the millennium for all
earthly inhabitants to see.[4] After the 1,000 years, God
will bring this Holy City down to the Earth where it will
reside for all the ages to come.

The beauty and splendor of this great city are pictured as
a bride adorned for her husband because it appeared as a
magnificent and brightly light city illuminated by the
glory of God and the Lamb.

# Reference Notes

**Prologue to Introduction**

**1)** The traditional site for the Sermon on the Mount, where all of the tour buses stop, is located near the Sea of Galilee in a beautiful little chapel known as the Church of the Beatitudes. The actual site where Jesus delivered His famous sermon was on the Mount of Beatitudes, which is located roughly a mile or so from the sea. For a picture of this famous site, please see our book on the Sermon on the Mount, entitled ***Overcomers' Guide to the Kingdom***, available at: www.ProphecyCountdown.com

**2)** Panton, D.M. – ***Judgment Seat of Christ***, Schoettle Publishing Co., p. 17.

**Chapter 1 – Salvation: Past, Present and Future**

**1)** Chambers, Oswald – ***My Utmost for His Highest 1996 Personal Planner***, Vision House Publishing Inc. © 1996, reading for February 5-11, 1996: The Cost of Sanctification.

**Chapter 2 – Cost of Sanctification**

**1)** Mauro, Philip – ***God's Pilgrims***, Schoettle Publishing Co. Inc., © 1984, p. 136. (Emphasis by Mauro in his writings). Philip Mauro was a foremost attorney who came to Christ at age 49. He is most noted for writing the brief that William Jennings Bryan used to win the famous Tennessee-Scopes trial (evolution) in 1925. While his work as a lawyer was impressive, the Lord also used his writing talents to communicate teachings from the Bible. In ***God's Pilgrims***, he skillfully explains one of the least understood teachings in today's Church: *the salvation of the soul*. Please see Appendix 4 for an excerpt from his book.

**2)** *Justification by works* was taught by our Lord because He wants to reward those believers who have diligently been obedient to His teachings. The book of James also teaches on the subject of *justification by works*, which is covered in chapters 3 and 4 of this book.

**Chapter 3 – Receive the Implanted Word**

**1)** Matthew Henry Commentary on Malachi 3:1-6.

## Chapter 3 – Receive the Implanted Word

**2)** Mize, Lyn – ***Book of James***, © n/a, which is available on his website at: www.ffwfthb.org

## Chapter 5 – Goal of Our Faith

**1)** Soteriological salvation is salvation from hell, i.e. from damnation in the Lake of Fire. Soteriology is based upon two biblical Greek words, *soteria* (salvation) and *logos* (teaching), and the term refers to biblical doctrines of salvation.

**2)** The Apostle Paul gives us many examples, which should have a sobering effect upon those Christians who are not truly being led by the Spirit of God, and are in danger of losing their inheritance in the Kingdom:

*"So I say, live by the Spirit, and you will not gratify the desires of the sinful nature...The acts of the sinful nature are obvious: sexual immorality, impurity and debauchery; idolatry and witchcraft; hatred, discord, jealousy, fits of rage, selfish ambition, dissensions, factions and envy; drunkenness, orgies, and the like. I warn you, as I did before, that those who live like this will not inherit the kingdom of God."* (Gal 5:16, 19-21 – NIV)

*"But among you there must not be even a hint of sexual immorality, or of any kind of impurity, or of greed, because these are improper for God's holy people. Nor should there be obscenity, foolish talk or coarse joking, which are out of place, but rather thanksgiving. For of this you can be sure: No immoral, impure or greedy person – such a man is an idolater – has any inheritance in the kingdom of Christ and of God. Let no one deceive you with empty words, for because of such things God's wrath comes on those who are disobedient."* (Eph 5:3-6 – NIV)

*"Since, then, you have been raised with Christ, set your hearts on things above, where Christ is seated at the right*

**Chapter 5 – Goal of Our Faith (continued)**

*hand of God. Set your minds on things above, not on earthly things. For you died, and your life is now hidden with Christ in God. When Christ, who is your life, appears, then you also will appear with him in glory. Put to death, therefore, whatever belongs to your earthly nature: sexual immorality, impurity, lust, evil desires and greed, which is idolatry. Because of these, the wrath of God is coming. You used to walk in these ways, in the life you once lived. But now you must rid yourselves of all such things as these: anger, rage, malice, slander, and filthy language from your lips. Do not lie to each other, since you have taken off your old self with its practices and have put on the new self, which is being renewed in knowledge in the image of its Creator."* (Col 3:1-10 – NIV)

**3)** Wuest, Kenneth S. – *The New Testament An Expanded Translation*, W. B. Eerdmans Publishing Company © 1961, p. 549

**4)** Please see author's book on Revelation: *Calling All Overcomers*, p.152, www.ProphecyCountdown.com

**Appendix 1 – The Crucified Life**

**1)** Hollandsworth, James S.–*Christ Magnified* © 2006, p. 25.

**2)** Ibid., p. 31.

**Appendix 2 – Overcomers**

**1)** Lang, G.H. – *The Revelation of Jesus Christ*, Schoettle Publishing © 2006, p. 91.

**2)** Govett, Robert – *Seek First His Kingdom and His Righteousness* Tract (please see the Supplemental Articles on our website for the entire Tract).

**Appendix 3 – The Prize of Our Calling**

**1)** Panton, D.M., op.cit, pp. 57-61. D.M. Panton's excellent book entitled *The Judgment Seat of Christ* is this author's favorite book, which is highly recommended for all believers interested in learning more about this important subject. It can be purchased from the Schoettle Publishing Company, P.O. Box 1246, Hayesville, NC 28904, www.schoettlepublishing.com

## Well Done
### by The Afters

What will it be like when my pain is gone
And all the worries of this world just fade away?
What will it be like when You call my name
And that moment when I see You face to face?
I'm waiting my whole life to hear You say

Well done, well done
My good and faithful one
Welcome to the place where you belong
Well done, well done
My beloved child

You have run the race and now you're home
Welcome to the place where you belong
What will it be like when tears are washed away
And every broken thing will finally be made whole?
What will it be like when I come into Your glory
Standing in the presence of a love so beautiful?
I'm waiting my whole life for that day
I will live my life to hear You say

Well done, well done
My good and faithful one
Welcome to...

© 2018 The Afters. All Rights Reserved.

To view a recent YouTube video of this beautiful song, please see the
*Supplemental Articles* section for *Salvation of the Soul* on our
website (www.ProphecyCountdown.com).

# Bibliography

## References Consulted

Benware, Paul N. – *The Believer's Payday*, AMG Publishers, © 2002 **

Cauley, Marty A – *Rewards are Eternal*, Misthological Press, © 2015 * (*** for advanced students)

Chambers, Oswald – *My Utmost for His Highest 1996 Personal Planner*, Vision House Publishing, Inc. © 1996

Chambers, Oswald – *Studies in the Sermon on the Mount*, Forgotten Books (Original London: Simpkin Marshall, Ltd.)

Chitwood, Arlen L. – *Salvation of the Soul*, The Lamp Broadcast, Inc. © 2011* (*** for advanced students)

Crawford, Scott – *Hebrews: The Five Warnings for Believers*, Word of Truth Press, © 2006 ***

Crawford, Scott – *Perseverance Pays: Winning the Crown of Life*, Word of Truth Press, © 2011 ***

Dines, Charlie – *Being Glorified Together With Him: The Reward of the Inheritance*, © 2012 **

Govett, Robert – *Govett On John*, Schoettle Publishing Co. Inc, © 2010, www.schoettlepublishing.com

Hodges, Zane C. – *The Epistle of James*, Grace Evangelical Society © 2009

Hollandsworth, James S. – *Christ Magnified: Glorifying Jesus by Your Life*, Hollypublishing © 2006 ***

Hollandsworth, James S. – *The End of the Pilgrimage*, Hollypublishing © 2015 ***

Lang, G.H. – *The Revelation of Jesus Christ*, Schoettle Publishing © 2006, www.schoettlepublishing.com ***

Larkin, Rev. Clarence – *Dispensational Truth*, Rev. Clarence Larkin Estate © 1918-1922. Pictures shown in this book are used with permission of the Rev. Clarence Larkin Estate: P.O. Box 334, Glenside, PA 19038, USA, * 215-576-5590, www.larkinestate.com

## References Consulted (continued)

Lutzer, Erwin W. – *Your Eternal Reward: Triumph and Tears at the Judgment Seat of Christ*, Moody Press © 1998 **

Mauro, Philip – *God's Pilgrims*, Schoettle Publishing Co. Inc., © 1984, www.schoettlepublishing.com **

Missler, Chuck and Nancy – *The Kingdom, Power and Glory*, The King's High Way Ministries, Inc. © 2009 **

Missler, Nancy – *Reflections of His Image,* The King's High Way Ministries, Inc. © 2006 ***

Mize, Lyn – *The Open Door*, Meat in Due Season Ministries, © 1994 ***

Nee, Watchman – *The Salvation of the Soul*, Christian Fellowship Publishers, Inc., © 1978 **

Panton, D. M. – *The Judgment Seat of Christ*, Schoettle Publishing Co. Inc., © 1984 ***
Excerpts shown in Appendix 3 are used with permission of Schoettle Publishing Co., P.O. Box 1246, Hayesville, NC 28904, (706) 896-3333, www.schoettlepublishing.com

Shupe, Pastor Randy – *The Glory of His Inheritance: The Bride of Christ* © 1988, www.PastorRandyShupe.com ***

Whipple, Gary T. – *Beyond the Rapture: Shock and Surprise*, Schoettle Publishing Co. Inc., © 1984 **

Wuest, Kenneth S. – *The New Testament An Expanded Translation*, W.B. Eerdmans Publishing Company © 1961*

* Most useful reference sources in this author's opinion.

---

**NOTE TO READER**

One of the purposes of this current title is to whet the believer's appetite for a deeper study into the important subject of the *salvation of the soul* and preparation for the *Judgment Seat of Christ*. The above resources should be helpful in preparing readers for the most important day when we stand before the Lord.

# ABBREVIATIONS

## Books of the Bible

### Old Testament (OT)

Genesis (Gen)                Ecclesiastes (Ecc)
Exodus (Exd)                 Solomon (Sgs)
Leviticus (Lev)              Isaiah (Isa)
Numbers (Num)                Jeremiah (Jer)
Deuteronomy (Deu)            Lamentations (Lam)
Joshua (Jos)                 Ezekiel (Eze)
Judges (Jdg)                 Daniel (Dan)
Ruth (Rth)                   Hosea (Hsa)
1 Samuel (1Sa)               Joel (Joe)
2 Samuel (2Sa)               Amos (Amo)
1 Kings (1Ki)                Obadiah (Oba)
2 Kings (2Ki)                Jonah (Jon)
1 Chronicles (1Ch)           Micah (Mic)
2 Chronicles (2Ch)           Nahum (Nah)
Ezra (Ezr)                   Habakkuk (Hab)
Nehemiah (Neh)               Zephaniah (Zep)
Esther (Est)                 Haggai (Hag)
Job (Job)                    Zechariah (Zec)
Psalms (Psa)                 Malachi (Mal)
Proverbs (Pro)

### New Testament (NT)

Matthew (Mat)                1 Timothy (1Ti)
Mark (Mar)                   2 Timothy (2Ti)
Luke (Luk)                   Titus (Tts)
John (Jhn)                   Philemon (Phm)
Acts (Act)                   Hebrews (Hbr)
Romans (Rom)                 James (Jam)
1 Corinthians (1Cr)          1 Peter (1Pe)
2 Corinthians (2Cr)          2 Peter (2Pe)
Galatians (Gal)              1 John (1Jo)
Ephesians (Eph)              2 John (2Jo)
Philippians (Phl)            3 John (3Jo)
Colossians (Col)             Jude (Jud)
1 Thessalonians (1Th)        Revelation (Rev)
2 Thessalonians (2Th)

As Jesus carried the cross that He died upon: John 19:17, believers are to take up their cross and follow Him: Matthew 16:24.

# Appendix 1 – The Crucified Life

*I have been crucified with Christ; it is no longer I who live,*
*but Christ lives in me; and the life which I now live in the flesh*
*I live by faith in the Son of God,*
*who loved me and gave Himself for me.* (Gal 2:20)

Every born-again Christian is given a new nature at his spiritual rebirth. Since this new nature is born of God, it is completely sinless and in tune with the Holy Spirit. This new *spirit* nature is the person or *"whosoever"* in the following:

> **Whosoever** *is born of God doth not commit sin;*
> *for his seed remaineth in him: and* **he cannot sin,**
> *because* **he is born of God.** (1John 3:9 – KJV)

This is saying that the Christian does not continue sinning in the realm of our *spirit* because we have been born of God. This wonder took place in our *spirit* the moment we were saved.

> *Knowing this, that our* **old man** *was crucified with Him,*
> *that the body of sin* <u>might</u> *be done away with, that we*
> **should** *no longer be slaves to sin.* (Rom 6:6)

While the *"old man"* is dead (it has been crucified), our *soul* still has the same propensities to sin because of our flesh nature (*the body of sin*). The power of sin in our life keeps tugging at us to sin.

While repentance and baptism are not requirements for the new birth experience, they are requirements for the Christian to become a faithful Christian. **Repentance is a work** that every Christian should do after he has been born-again, but it does not precede spirit salvation. The Gospel of John was written about spiritual regeneration and the mission of Christ as the Son of God. The word "repent" or "repentance" is not found in the Gospel of John.

Belief or faith in the atoning sacrifice of Jesus Christ is the natural and certain response to spiritual regeneration, but repentance is an act of obedience. After spiritual regeneration, the Holy Spirit convicts every Christian about his sinful state, and he is commanded to repent and be baptized. Repentance means to turn away from sin (change of mind). It means that the Christian should become a follower or disciple of Christ.

Baptism is a ritual or ordinance of God that symbolizes that a Christian has chosen to follow Christ. Baptism symbolizes death and resurrection and means that the Christian has committed himself to dying to the flesh and living according to righteousness. It means the Christian has committed himself to studying the Bible and living according to its precepts or teachings. It means the Christian has chosen to seek the Kingdom of God with all of his heart, mind and soul. It means the Christian has decided to give up his old way of life for a new life. It means the Christian has counted the costs of giving up his old life, and living a new life in obedience to the Word of God. It means the Christian has committed to **losing his soul** now in this life, so that he can **save his soul** at the Judgment Seat of Christ. This is confirmed in the following Scripture:

*24) Then said Jesus **unto his disciples**, If any man will come after me, let him deny himself, and take up his cross, and follow me. 25) For whosoever will save his life (i.e., soul) shall lose it: and whosoever will lose his life (i.e., soul) for my sake shall find it. 26) For what is a man profited, if he shall gain the whole world, and lose his own soul? or what shall a man give in exchange for his soul? 27) For the Son of man shall come in the glory of his Father with his angels;*
*and then he shall **reward** every man according to his works.*
(Matthew 16:24-27 – KJV)

The above passage of Scripture establishes conclusively that the Christian must do something other than believing in Christ to save his soul. It also establishes with certainty that soul salvation is something that believers must seek after. It also clearly establishes that soul salvation is in accordance with works and the REWARD for the Christian's life. The Christian must lose his soul or life, in order to save it at the Judgment Seat of Christ.

There are many Christians that hear the gospel of grace, believe in the atoning death of Jesus Christ, but they are never obedient to the command to repent and be baptized. Many Christians go through the motions of repentance and baptism, but they do not follow through with this commitment. Many were probably sincere in their commitment, but they failed to count the costs of this commitment. These Christians are still saved spiritually and they will be with God for eternity, but they fail to allow Christ to crucify their lives.

> *I have been crucified with Christ; it is no longer I who live, but Christ lives in me; and the life which I now live in the flesh I live by faith in the Son of God, who loved me and gave Himself for me.* (Gal 2:20)

Living the crucified life requires dying to self on a daily basis and allowing the Holy Spirit to live His life in us. By yielding our lives to Christ, we are able to appropriate His mighty power and thereby overcome the power of sin in our lives.

As pointed out by James Hollandsworth: "If sin is ruling you, then you have not exchanged your life for His life. That's a tragedy, for the Holy Spirit of God who lives within you is eager to enable you to obey God."[1]

Many try to obtain the victory over sin in their life by relying upon themselves. Self effort does not work because we do not hold the power to win the battle by ourselves. Only by yielding and surrendering our life to Him, by dying to self, can we appropriate His mighty power in us to obtain the victory over our fleshly carnal nature.

> *1) There is therefore now no condemnation to those who are in Christ Jesus, who do not walk according to the flesh, but according to the Spirit. 4) that the righteous requirement of the law might be fulfilled in us who do* **not walk according to the flesh but according to the Spirit** *(Rom 8:1,4).*

Yielding our life to the Holy Spirit is a daily decision we must make in order to allow Him control of our life, and thereby win the battle. The key to our victory is depending upon Christ to live His life in us.

Living the crucified life is what being a Christian is really about. By allowing Christ to live His life in us, we will daily die to self, giving Him the opportunity to use our lives to glorify Him. James Hollandsworth captures this truth in the following brief story.

> One day as I was driving along the interstate, I noticed along the side of the road a small cross in the grass with some flowers around it and on the cross, a name inscribed. Apparently, someone had lost a loved one in a vehicle accident at that very place, and that was their way of remembering and honoring. But the blessed paradox of Galatians 2:20 is that in a spiritual sense we should have many such crosses along the road of life, signaling the daily death of self. We should be able to look back and remember numerous crosses, signifying all the times we died to self by choosing to depend on Christ so that He might live through us. What a joy those crosses bring, as they represent dying so that we might truly live.[2]

# Appendix 2 – Overcomers

One of the main purposes of this book is to help Christians become the overcomers God wants us to be. Many of the teachings taught in the church today are based upon human tradition.

Paul gives us a strong warning about "Tradition" as shown in the following translations of Colossians 2:8:

*Beware lest any man spoil you through philosophy and vain deceit, after the tradition of men, after the rudiments of the world, and not after Christ. (KJV)*
*See to it that no one takes you captive through hollow and deceptive philosophy, which depends on human tradition and the basic principles of this world rather than on Christ. (NIV)*

Traditions come about through human philosophy that can cause us to completely miss what God is telling us. One of the popular teachings in today's church is that all Christians are automatically "overcomers" when they become a believer. While we love Mandisa's catchy hit tune: ***Overcomer***, we would take exception to the implication that we are automatically overcomers. Rather than singing, *"You're an overcomer,"* we would change the lyrics slightly to: *"Be an overcomer."*

Being an overcomer is what being a Christian is all about. Granted, accepting Christ is vital to becoming an overcomer, it is really only the first step.

*For whatsoever is born of God overcometh the world: and this is the victory that overcometh the world, even our faith. Who is he that overcometh the world, but he that believeth that Jesus is the Son of God? (1Jo 5:4-5)*

The first two times the word "*overcometh*" is used is found in the above Scripture. John is telling us that only those who are born of God, and believe that Jesus is the Son of God, have overcome the world by their faith. All that is required to overcome the world is the believer's faith in Jesus Christ.

### Overcome the Flesh and the Devil
But, to be considered a successful overcomer at the Judgment Seat of Christ, the Christian also must also be able to overcome the flesh and overcome the devil.

> *For all that is in the world, the lust of the flesh,*
> *and the lust of the eyes, and the pride of life,*
> *is not of the Father, but is of the world.* (1 Jo 2:16)

> *For we wrestle not against flesh and blood,*
> *but against principalities, against powers,*
> *against the rulers of the darkness of this world,*
> *against spiritual wickedness in high places.* (Eph 6:12)

Once a person receives Christ as their personal Saviour, they overcome the world by their faith in Jesus. At this point, a battle begins for the believer's soul. The flesh wants to gratify itself and the devil will attempt to destroy the new Christian's soul. Remember, the whole goal of our faith is the salvation of our soul: *"Receiving the end of your faith, even the salvation of your souls"* (1 Pe 1:9).

In order to be a successful overcomer at the Judgment Seat of Christ, the Christian needs to ensure that his *soul* is saved by winning the victory over his flesh and the devil. Remember that your *spirit* was saved when you believed in Christ. The salvation of the *soul* requires the defeat of the world, the flesh and the devil. Only once all three are defeated will the Christian be considered a true overcomer. This requires a daily victory that won't end until life's journey is complete.

The world, our flesh and the devil will attempt to defeat us every single day. In order to be successful overcomers we must learn to continually die to self and allow the Holy Spirit to direct and empower our lives. In order to be an overcomer, we must continually seek the Lord's help, realizing that relying on our own strength will not work:

*I am the vine, you are the branches. He who abides in Me, and I in him, bears much fruit; for without Me you can do nothing.*
(Jhn 15:5)

The overcomer learns to place his life in Christ's hands, and only by abiding in Jesus and being filled with the Holy Spirit can we exhibit the fruit of his life to this fallen world.

*28) Come to Me, all you who labor and are heavy laden, and I will give you rest. 29) Take My yoke upon you and learn from Me, for I am gentle and lowly in heart, and you will find rest for your souls. 30) For My yoke is easy and My burden is light.*
(Mat 11:28-30)

---

**Learning to be an overcomer is perhaps the most difficult thing to do on this earth as a human being. The overcomer is born through the victory they receive by trusting in Jesus Christ.**

To learn more on the subject of what being an overcomer is all about, the reader is encouraged to see the author's previous trilogy of books on the important subject of being an overcomer: ***The Kingdom, Overcomers' Guide to the Kingdom*** and ***Calling All Overcomers***. All three of these books may be freely downloaded from our website to save on your computer and to share with all your close friends, relatives and loved ones: www.ProphecyCountdown.com

*Excerpt from THE COMING SPIRITUAL EARTHQUAKE*

An overcomer is a believer who has had an authentic experience with God. Though thrown into the furnace of affliction, they have come forth as pure gold. The overcomer is born through the victory they receive by trusting in Jesus Christ. Learning to be an overcomer is perhaps the most difficult thing to do on this earth as a human being. Possessing impressive credentials and degrees offer little solace when it comes to where the "rubber meets the road." Every professing Christian must learn to be an overcomer through faith and total trust in their Savior. In Matthew 11:28-30, Jesus urges: *"Come unto me, all ye that labour and are heavy laden, and I will give you rest. Take my yoke upon you, and learn of me; for I am meek and lowly in heart: and ye shall find rest unto your souls. For my yoke is easy, and my burden is light."* The overcomers take their agony and burdens to the mighty counselor. Through prayer and trust, Jesus leads the downcast believer to "green pasture." The sting of the adversary is somehow turned to sweet victory. Christ alone is able to provide the peace that passes all understanding. While every believer will have trials and testing in this world, Christ reminded us to be of good cheer because He overcame this world. As believers, we find our sweet victory in Him! Overcomers are believers who find their strength and help in Him--not through man, but by the power of the Son of God. A genuine overcomer follows in Christ's footsteps. They learn to "take it on the chin" and to "take it to the cross." Whatever the world dishes out is handled with prayer and placed on the altar before God. By offering everything to Christ, they find hope and sufficiency in Him. Being an overcomer is what being a Christian is all about. Through the trials of this life, the overcomers' faith is put on trial and thereby confirmed as Holy evidence before a mighty God, it is authentic. As our example, Jesus endured the cross for the joy set before Him. Overcomers have the victory because of His victory. Through His victory, the overcomer is able to walk in newness of life. The overcomer knows: they have been crucified with Christ and their old life is gone (Gal 2:20). By dying to self, the overcomer experiences the joy of Christ's triumph in their life. Finally, an overcomer is grateful and humble: for they know of God's rich mercy and marvelous grace. If it wasn't for Christ, they would be doomed. Out of this gratitude, rises the song of gladness and praise. An overcomers' heart bursts forth with praise and adoration unto their God for the victory He provides. The overcomer knows, first hand, that while weeping may endure for the night: joy cometh in the morning!

"The assertion that all believers are overcomers is so plainly contrary to fact and to Scripture that one wonders it ever has been made. It involves the false position that no believer can be a backslider. It avoids and nullifies the solemn warnings and urgent pleadings of the Spirit addressed to believers, and, by depriving Christians of these, leaves him dangerously exposed to the perils they reveal."[1]

G. H. Lang
***The Revelation of Jesus Christ***

"It has been pointed out that the Lord names overcomers in every one of His seven letters to the Churches (Panton). What a remarkable encouragement and revelation is this fact, especially for those of us who have been overcome, and have failed Him so often in the past! If we repent, and honestly and genuinely seek His help and strength to obey His word, we also can be overcomers. Let's not allow ourselves to be side-tracked by those 'who consider reward to be beneath the notice of a CHRISTIAN.' Let's be like Paul and *"press on toward the goal to win the prize..."* (Phil. 3:14)[2]

Robert Govett
***Seek First His Kingdom and His Righteousness*** (Tract)

*"Run in such a way as to get the prize."*
1 Corinthians 9:24

# Appendix 3 – The Prize of Our Calling

*Wherefore **we labour**, that, whether present or absent, we **may be accepted of him**. 10) **For we must all appear before the judgment seat of Christ; that every one may receive the things done in his body, according to that he hath done, whether it be good or bad. 11) Knowing therefore the terror of the Lord, we persuade men**. (2Cr 5:9-11 – KJV)*

One of the greatest incentives for Christians to live godly lives is a knowledge and understanding of the Judgment Seat of Christ. The Judgment Seat of Christ is probably one of the least understood topics in Scripture. Numerous Christians have the vague idea that they will appear at this judgment in order to determine if they have been saved. The very popular traditional understanding about this judgment has Jesus asking someone why He should allow him into heaven. The supposedly correct answer is because the person has received Jesus Christ. This traditional teaching is not accurate, since everyone who appears at this judgment has believed in the atoning sacrifice of Jesus Christ. Every Christian's spirit salvation will have already been determined, or he would not be at the Judgment Seat of Christ.

The Judgment Seat of Christ is a judgment of the works of each believer to determine the rewards that each one will receive. Since every Christian will appear before this Judgment Seat, it is imperative for all believers to live their life with this in mind.

D.M. Panton's excellent book: *The Judgment Seat of Christ* discusses this subject in great detail. Beginning on page 57, he discusses what he believes Paul was referring to regarding the *"prize"* all Christians should be striving for in 1 Corinthians 9:24. He believes this *"prize"* represents the "Kingdom" and the believer's qualification to rule and reign with Christ:

### The Prize of Our Calling

We are now in the position to summarize our conclusions concerning entry into the Millennial Kingdom. Is the Kingdom – as well as rank in it – the Prize for which the Christian is to run, and which may be forfeited, unless a standard of holiness be attained known only to God? **It is so –**

1. Because our Lord states in the Gospels, the Holy Spirit repeats it in nearly every Epistle, it is the basis of the promises and threats to the Seven Churches, and it is foretold as and actual experience in the prophecies of the Apocalypse.

2. Because the Types of the Old Testament, largely an unquarried mine, strikingly corroborate it, thus confirming our understanding of the literal passages of the New Testament, and weaving all into an exquisite mosaic of revelation.

3. Because the Age to Come – as distinct from the Eternal State, which is based on grace alone (Rev. 20:15) is revealed as "one last day of a thousand years, a full and perfect judicial aeon," in which all seed sown in this Age reaps its exactly corresponding harvest, and to which all adverse consequences of works done after faith are confined.

4. Because it safeguards the infinite merits of our Lord's imputed righteousness and divine sacrifice by establishing the spotless and eternal standing of every believer in Him while it also safeguards human responsibility and divine justice by making every believer accountable for his walk, under pain of possible forfeiture of coming glory.

5. Because – since God's dealings with His people must always rest on the character of God, and God's character is not mercy only, but justice also – it is inconceivable that a disciple's life, if

unholy, should have no profounder effect on his destiny than mere gradation in glory.

6.  Because, if we acknowledge any judgment of a believer's works at all, and that before a tribunal which is a *judgment* seat and not a *mercy* seat, we are thereby compelled to acknowledge, further, that the investigation must be strictly judicial, and that it will therefore be as exactly graded in censure as it is in praise.

7.  Because it vindicates the holiness and justice of God from the charge of compounding with His people's sins, and makes the highest glory given by God to rest only on the active righteousness of the disciple co-operating, consistently and ceaselessly, with the imputed righteousness of his Lord, - obedience being the only proof of love.

8.  Because it is the supreme reconciliation between Paul and James – that is, between justification through faith unto Eternal Life and justification through works unto Millennial Reward; for into and Everlasting Kingdom, which is granted as a gift, and abundant entrance can only be a prior one, and it is built upon a sevenfold foundation of works (II Peter 1:5-11).

(1) Before works: Rom. 4:10, Gen. 15:6
(2) After works: James 2:21, Gen. 22:16

9.  Because it is perhaps as near an approximation as has yet been reached to a solution of the perennial controversy between the Calvinist and the Arminian: for it establishes all the passages of glorious certainty, while it leaves ample scope for the most solemn warnings: it takes both sets of Scripture as it finds them.

10.  Because it gives the natural and unforced interpretation to the facts of Church life, as it does also to the simple statements of Holy Writ, and reveals how exactly the one squares with the

other, both in present character and in just recompense; and whether as selective rapture, or exclusive resurrection, or forfeiture of crowns, or failure of the prize, or conflagration of works, or limited coheirship or even penal consequences – the argument is cumulative, and overwhelming in its accumulation.

11. Because large sections of the Church of God are purged, and can only be purged, by seeing the drastic consequences of a carnal life; and because, for want of a frank and fearless statement of these consequences, multitudes of disciples are now wrapt in profound slumber.

12. Because it purges every motive with the awful vision of the Judgment Seat of Christ, and supplies an incentive second only to the love in its motive power for alienating the disciple from the world and filling him with a passion for the Kingdom of God; and because it is the golden possibility for every child of God to share Messiah's Throne."

Panton's analysis that the "prize" represents the believer's entry into the Kingdom and his rule and reign with Jesus Christ should motivate all Christians to examine their walk with the Lord. Our salvation is a free gift provided by God's grace; however, our rewards represent God's recompense for our faithfulness.

When we stand before the Lord, all Christians want to be able to hear Him say: ***"Well done, thou good and faithful servant…"*** but many may be given a rebuke by Jesus and have *"shame at His coming"* (1 John 2:28). This should motivate everyone to live their life pleasing to the Lord as they ***"run in such a way as to get the prize"*** (1 Corinthians 9:24).

The above excerpt is from ***The Judgment Seat of Christ,*** by D.M. Panton, pages 57-61, © 1984. Used with permission of the Schoettle Publishing Co., www.schoettlepublishing.com

# Appendix 4 – Saving the Soul (Philip Mauro)

**SAVING THE SOUL**. We are not aware that anyone has heretofore attempted to lead the Lord's people to inquire precisely what is meant by *saving the soul*. So far as we have information, it is a new subject; and it is very probable that most of our readers have never sought to trace, by the aid of the Scriptures, the distinction between *soul* and *spirit*. It is not surprising, therefore, that some have found difficulty in laying hold of that distinction. Desiring to aid further to that end, we offer here some additional suggestions.

The point of chief importance to be grasped is that "saving the *soul*" does not mean escaping eternal perdition. The saving of the *soul* is not what is preached as the Gospel of God's grace to sinners. What the Gospel offers to every believing sinner is the *forgiveness of sins* and the bestowal of *eternal life* as the free-gift of God. Hence the saving of the *soul* is never spoken of in connection with the Gospel. It is not in the Lord's commission to the apostles (Luke 24:47). It is not in Peter's addresses to Jews in Acts 2 and 3, and to Gentiles in Acts 10. It is not in Paul's model Gospel address in Acts 13, nor in his Epistles which treat of the Gospel (Rom., Cor., Gal.).

The saving of the *soul* is something radically different from the justification and life which God bestows upon every sinner who believes on the Crucified and Risen Savior. The saving of the *soul* is **not preached to sinners at all**. It is spoken of by the Lord only to His disciples, and by the apostles only to believers. Moreover it is invariably spoken of as something in regard to which the saints themselves have responsibility.

Losing one's *soul* does not mean being eternally lost, i.e., damned. It does not mean incurring the wrath of God. Conclusive proof of this is furnished by the Lord's words to

His disciples in whom  He  urged them,  for their  own
advantage, to lose their own *souls*, and to hate their own
*souls* in  this world. We need hardly say the Lord did not
exhort His disciples to be damned in this world. If losing the
*soul* in this world does not mean damnation, then losing it in
the world to come does  not mean damnation.

On the other hand, we may learn what is meant by saving
the *soul* in the world to come, by ascertaining what it means
for a man to "find his *soul*" in this present world; and this we
may  do  by  attentively  considering  the  Scriptures  cited  in
chapter 16 of this book. Whatever is meant by  finding one's
*soul* in this age, the same thing is meant by finding it in the age
to come.

By reference to those Scriptures it will be seen that the subject
of saving and losing the *soul* is  always  found in connection
with a  reference  to experiences in this world that are  directly
contrary to the natural feelings and desires of a human being,
and which involve present loss, suffering, trial, or *denial of self*
in  some  form.  The  first  occurrence  of  the  subject  is  in
connection with the  sufferings  which  the  Lord  foretold as
awaiting the twelve (Matt. 10:16-39). The next is in connection
with the Lord's disclosure to His disciples of the sufferings that
awaited  Himself  at  Jerusalem  (Matt.  16:21-27).  He  was
speaking there of laying down His own Soul, and His call to
His disciples is to "follow" Him in losing ***their*** souls in this
world, though not necessarily in the  same manner in which He
parted with His.

 Likewise in John 12:23-27 the Lord speaks of saving and
losing the *soul* in direct connection  with His own Sufferings
on the  Cross. And here it is recorded that He used the
expression "Now  is My SOUL troubled."

In Luke 21:19 the Lord's exhortation "By your patience
(endurance) gain ye your *souls*" is found  in connection with

the sufferings which He foresaw for His disciples. By enduring those sufferings as the present portion of their *souls*, in lieu of the pleasures which the *soul* naturally craves, they were to "gain" their souls, though apparently losing them. In Heb.10 and 1 Pet. 1, where the same subject is referred to, the immediate context speaks of sufferings experienced through the natural human feelings. These Scriptures afford much light as to the significance of the expression we are considering.

Thus, from the teaching of the Lord and His Apostles, we learn that to every Christian is presented a choice between two paths in this world. One is the path of *self pleasing*. Those who take it are in pursuit of pleasures, honors, indulgences, and whatever else is gratifying to the natural feelings of a man, which feelings have their seat in his *soul*. There may be nothing inherently wrong in the things sought.

They may be quite proper and respectable, so that the Christian may "see no harm in them." In that path, then, one may perhaps succeed in finding gratifications for his *soul*, so far as it is possible for this present world to supply them. This is what we understand by "finding one's *soul* in this world."

The other path is that of *denial of one's self*. To walk in it involves submitting to present loss, to the daily cutting off of the *soul* from the things which exist in the world for its enjoyment. It involves the endurance of reproach, ridicule, and it may be of persecution, for Christ's sake and the Gospel's.

They who enter upon that path have deliberately **willed** (for it is an action of the heart) to part with their *souls*, as it were, during this present time for the sake of Christ. They "will" to lose their souls in this world; for the loss of the things that satisfy the *soul* of man is virtually the loss of the *soul* itself.

To choose that path is an act of *faith*; for the choice is influenced solely by the Word of God. Such a choice is, from the natural standpoint, an act of folly—throwing one's life away—for that path leads away from all that makes life in this world agreeable. They who walk in that path of separation and loss "walk by faith;" for they are influenced in so doing by "things not seen."

In fact, they must go directly against all the powerful attractions of the things that are seen. To follow the Word of God in a direction *contrary to nature*, and *because of what God has spoken*, is the walk of FAITH.

This is that particular kind of faith spoken of in Hebrews. Abraham displayed it when, at the bidding of God's Word, he came out of his native country, and when he sojourned as a stranger in the land promised to him for an inheritance (Heb. 11). This following of God's Word in a direction contrary to the natural inclinations, is the distinguishing trait of those who are "of faith to saving the *soul*;" for thereby they are distinguished from those who "draw back" to the resources of the world, seemingly to their immediate gain, but really to their great and irreparable loss (Heb. 10:39).

The Lord's words found in Matt. 11:29 are sufficiently clear to settle the meaning of the expression "saving the soul;" and surely no one who believes His words would dare, in the face of that saying, to maintain that a man can find rest unto his soul in any other way than by taking voluntarily the yoke of Christ upon Him, and by learning of Him meekness and lowliness of heart.

Finally, let us keep in view the main thing, which is, not to settle the meaning of a disputed passage of Scripture, but to secure the benefit of the doctrine of the Lord. Beyond all doubt, consequences of the most serious character depend upon our walk here below. Whether we describe those consequences by the words "saving the *soul*," or by some other words, does not affect their serious character. Whatever explanation of those disputed passages may seem right to us, we cannot afford to neglect that salvation so great, which at first began to be spoken by the Lord, and was confirmed unto us by them that heard Him (Mauro, pp.166-9).

> To take up the cross means to accept whatever God has decided for the person and to be willing to suffer according to the will of God. By denying self and taking up the cross we may truly follow the Lord.
> Watchman Nee

**From the Preface**

An interesting anecdote regarding Philip Mauro's book is found in its Preface: "It may be of interest to the reader to learn that the writing of this book was begun and finished on the memorable voyage of the Steamship *Carpathia* which was interrupted by the rescue of the survivors of the Titanic, and by the return with them to the port in New York....But that event – the sudden and dramatic over-throw of the latest and greatest human achievement of its kind, the ***most conspicuous object*** in the world – which stirred all Christendom to an unprecedented degree, served to impress powerfully upon the writer's mind the truth that the day is at hand for the shaking of all things, when the loftiness of man shall be bowed down, and the haughtiness of men shall be made low; and they shall go into the holes of the rocks, and into the caves of the earth for fear of the Lord and for the glory of His majesty, when He ariseth to shake terribly the earth. The destruction of the ***Titanic*** is a foreshadowing of what is about to happen to the great "civilization" upon which man has expended his energies, and in which he puts his confidence. For the unconverted, the obvious lesson of this tragic event is to ***inquire concerning the lifeboat***. But there are also solemn and important lessons in it for the saints of God. Some of these lessons the writer has endeavoured to set forth in the following pages.

SS. *Carpathia*, May 2, 1912 (Emphasis added by Mauro).

The above excerpts came from the Preface and the Appendix in ***God's Pilgrims,*** by Philip Mauro, pages 6-7, and 166-169. Used with the permission of the Schoettle Publishing Co., Inc. This book may be purchased at: www.schoettlepublishing.com This important book devotes an entire chapter to the ***salvation of the soul***, which is must reading for the Church today.

# Appendix 5 – God's Promise of Rewards

Many Christians in the church today are unfamiliar with or spurn God's system of rewards for His faithful ones. Christians have been so focused on the *past aspect of our salvation* that they have completely overlooked the *present/ongoing aspect of our salvation* and the just recompense of reward that goes along with this. Both aspects are of equal importance, and one must not be overemphasized to the total exclusion of the other.

It is because of this overemphasis on the past aspect of our salvation and the exclusion of the present aspect that the majority of Christians in the church today have very little understanding of the Kingdom of heaven, the accountability of Christians at the Judgment Seat of Christ, and the difference between *spirit* and *soul* salvation. All these are critical elements in our salvation, but the majority of Christians are not aware of these truths. God's promise of rewards has been greatly ignored by the churches in today's Laodicean age.

It is true that spirit salvation is by grace and grace alone. The Scriptures, which summarize salvation by grace is as follows:

> *8) For by grace are ye saved through faith; and that not of yourselves: it is the gift of God: 9) Not of works, lest any man should boast.* (Eph 2:8-9 – KJV)

The above two verses address our salvation by grace, but the following verse is usually ignored by Christians of all faiths. Verse 10 below addresses God's promise of rewards, and Christians are accountable for performing these *"good works."*

> *For we are his workmanship, created in Christ Jesus unto **good works**, which God hath before **ordained that we should walk in them**.* (Eph 2:10 – KJV)

All Christians will be judged at the Judgment Seat of Christ on how well we have been faithful. Numerous Scriptures address this accountability that Christians have for performing good works, but these Scriptures have been overlooked by many in the church today.

The primary example of confusing the Scriptures is the example of *soul* salvation. *Soul* salvation pertains to God's promise of rewards, and hundreds of Scriptures link *soul* salvation with our responsibility. Please see the introduction and chapter one for the differences. The primary Scripture for showing that *soul* salvation pertains to our obligation is as follows:

*Wherefore lay apart all filthiness and superfluity of naughtiness, and receive with meekness the engrafted word, which is able to save your souls.* (Jam 1:21 – KJV)

A second example of confusing the Scriptures pertains to the Kingdom of heaven. The issue of heaven or hell pertains to our salvation by grace, but the issue of entrance into the Kingdom of heaven pertains to God's promise of rewards. The following Scripture passage is the primary one for distinguishing entrance into the Kingdom of heaven—a rewards-related issue—from the new birth experience, which is related to grace:

*3) Jesus answered and said unto him, Verily, verily, I say unto thee, Except a man be born again, he cannot see*[1492] *the kingdom of God. 4) Nicodemus saith unto him, How can a man be born when he is old? can he enter the second time into his mother's womb, and be born?*

(*Eidō* (G 1492) To perceive, to know anything, understand.)

*5) Jesus answered, Verily, verily, I say unto thee, Except a man be born of water and of the Spirit, he cannot enter*[1525] *into the kingdom of God.* (Jhn 3:3-5 – KJV)

(*Eiserchomai* (G 1525) Entrance into, to go out or come in.)

Verse 3 above describes salvation by grace, and states that a person cannot comprehend the Kingdom of God unless he is born of God. Verse 5 describes God's promise of rewards by adding the additional criterion that one must be born of water in order to "*enter into the Kingdom of God.*" The phrase "*born of water*" has puzzled numerous students of the Bible and there is much debate over exactly what it means. Many think it means physical birth with the water referring to the amniotic fluid. Others think it means water baptism. The Church of Christ and several other denominations incorrectly think that water baptism is necessary for salvation in the evangelical sense. Finally others believe that it means the cleansing that Christ provides by "*the washing of water by the word...*"

The correct interpretation for the term "*born of water*" has both "literal" and "symbolic" meanings. "In the literal meaning, one must be born out of literal water and be immersed (the coming up portion of literal baptism)" (Whipple, p. 151). The requirement of water baptism pictures the death, burial and resurrection, which the believer shows by their act of obedience after being born again. Regarding the literal meaning, Robert Govett correctly pointed out:

> At first Jesus says, that 'Regeneration by the Spirit is absolutely necessary in order to *see* the Kingdom.' Nicodemus denies the possibility of a second birth. Then Jesus partially explains Himself. He adds to the birth of the Spirit – *the birth out of water*. The result is a stronger statement, on the other side, of the result of such birth. 'Except a man be born out *of water* and the Spirit, he cannot *enter into* the Kingdom of God." That is, the birth of *water* added on the one side, introduces *the entry* into the kingdom, on the other (Govett, p. 80).

In addition to the literal meaning of the term "*born of water,*" there is also a "symbolic" or "figurative" connotation. The "symbolic" meaning is shown by the following Scripture:

*25) Husbands, love your wives, even as Christ also loved the church, and gave himself for it; 26) That he might sanctify and cleanse it with the* **washing of water by the word***, 27) That he might present it to himself a glorious church, not having spot, or wrinkle, or any such thing; but that it should be holy and without blemish* (Eph 5:25-27 – KJV).

Please note the conditional aspects of verses 26 and 27. Christians who "***enter into the Kingdom of God***" must not only be born again but we must also be sanctified and cleansed by the "***washing of water by the word***." These are the Christians who study the Word of God and apply it to their lives, as described in chapter 3. Not all Christians do this, and not all Christians will become a partaker of this reward.

Progressive sanctification does not occur instantaneously as does the new birth experience (positional sanctification), but it takes a lifetime of faithful obedience to the Word of God. This is the "*renewing of the mind*" in Romans 12:2 and the "*perfecting holiness*" in 2 Corinthians 7:1. All Christians experience the new birth (i.e., they are justified), but all Christians are not being sanctified in the current pilgrim walk through the wilderness. Those who are faithful and obedient will be rewarded and be able to "enter the Kingdom of heaven."

The Kingdom of heaven pertains to the reign and rule of Jesus Christ in the coming kingdom, and only Christians who have been successful in realizing the salvation of their *soul* will realize this reward in the Kingdom of heaven. Heaven pertains to our salvation by grace, while the Kingdom of heaven pertains to promised rewards. Heaven is a place, but the Kingdom of heaven is a position of authority attained by faithfulness (see chapter 4). God's promise of rewards is central in the Scriptures, yet many Christians do not understand or have ignored this vital matter.

Esau lost his inheritance because he thought very little of it. Esau despised his birthright and sold it for a bowl of stew. Reuben gave up his inheritance for sensual pleasure with his father's concubine. Christians that disparage and ignore God's promise of rewards are also in danger of losing their inheritance in the Kingdom of heaven.

The phrase *"enter the Kingdom"* literally means to enter into the king's dominion, and it does not mean to enter into heaven. All Christians will enter heaven, but not all Christians will *"enter the Kingdom,"* since entrance into this aspect of the Kingdom is a privilege granted as a reward of our inheritance to those believers as described above and in chapter 5. Faithful believers will rule in the Holy City throughout eternity. Those believers who forfeit their rewards will lose this eternal privilege.

The chief differences between these two major aspects of our salvation can be summarized by the following chart:

| Past Aspect | Present/Ongoing |
|---|---|
| Salvation of the Spirit | Salvation of the Soul |
| Heaven | Kingdom of Heaven |
| Justified by Faith | Justified by Works |
| Faith Alone | Faithful Works |
| Free Gift | Earned Rewards |
| Guarantees Person Resides in Heaven | Guarantees Believer Kingdom of Heaven |
| Physical Place | Position of Authority |

Salvation is by grace, but rewards are according to works. The last words of Jesus recorded in the Scriptures are as follows:

*12) And, behold, I come quickly; and **my reward** is with me, **to give every man according as his work** shall be. 13) I am Alpha and Omega, the beginning and the end, the first and the last.*
(Rev 22:12-13 – KJV)

# How Long is a Generation?

*Now learn a parable of the fig tree; When his branch is yet tender, and putteth forth leaves, ye know that summer is nigh: So likewise ye, when ye shall see all these things, know that it is near, even at the doors. Verily I say unto you,* **This generation shall not pass, till all these things be fulfilled***.* (Mat 24:32-34 – KJV)

What was the average life expectancy at the time of Jesus?

Those living in the days of **Jesus** (as mentioned in the New Testament) had an **average life span** that was similar to human life spans before the arrival of modern medicine and technology. At the time Jesus spoke the above words, the **average life expectancy** was around 30 to 35 years, similar to the **life span** of those in classical Rome.

> 32 AD + 35 = 67 AD around the time that the Romans' siege of Jerusalem began (3½ years of judgment), ending in 70 AD.

In 1948 the average life expectancy was approximately 70 years (or 80 because of strength, as in Psalm 90).

> 1948 + 70 = 2018 + ?

*The days of our life are* **seventy years**— *Or even, if because of strength,* **eighty years***; Yet their pride [in additional years] is only labor and sorrow, For it is soon gone and we fly away.* (Psa 90:10 – AMP)

# Appendix 6 – Watching for Jesus

*Therefore let us not sleep, as others do,*
***but let us watch*** *and be sober.* (1Th 5:6)

The Word of God shows that Jesus is returning again the second time and we should be watching for His return. Are you looking for Jesus to come again? If not, now is the time to start your watch because it is much later than most people think.

We do not know for certain the exact time that Jesus will return. Just before Jesus left this earth the first time, he told His disciples that He was going to return and He commanded them to "*watch*." What does it mean to continue watching?

Some of the things "*watching*" entails include:

1) Being aware of the prophetic signs in God's Word.
2) Living a life of holiness before our Lord.
3) Living a life separated from the world.
4) Encouraging one another with the wonderful Hope of His soon return.
5) Telling others Jesus is coming soon and of their need to be ready.
6) Praying the prayer Jesus taught us to pray in Luke 21:

*And take heed to yourselves, lest at any time your hearts be overcharged with surfeiting, and drunkenness, and cares of this life, and so that day come upon you unawares. For like a snare shall it come on all them that dwell on the face of the whole earth. **Watch ye, therefore, and <u>pray always,</u> that ye may be accounted worthy to escape all these things that shall come to pass, and to stand before the Son of Man.***
(Luke 21:34-36 – KJV)

The act of *"watching"* is serious business with our Lord. If we fail to continue our diligence, Revelation 3:3 gives us fair warning:

> *Remember therefore how thou hast received and heard, and hold fast, and repent. If therefore **thou shalt not watch**, I will **come on thee as a thief**, and thou **shalt not know** what hour I will come upon thee.*
> (Rev 3:3 – KJV)

Those who are not *"watching"* will be taken by surprise since a thief comes unannounced. The wise and faithful followers of Jesus; however, will continue *"watching"* for Him and they will not be surprised. Begin *"watching"* today before it is too late! Jesus is coming, very, very soon!

Are you ready if Jesus returned today? If you are not sure, please consider making the following prayer right now:

> *"Dear God in Heaven, I realize that I have not really been living my life for You. I humbly turn to You right now and ask You to forgive me. Dear Jesus, please rule and reign in my heart and life. Please help me to live for You for whatever time remains. I pray that I may be ready and that I may be able to stand before You when You return for me. In Jesus' name I pray. Amen."*

Our prayer is that many in the Church will pray this prayer and ask the Lord to help them be prepared for His return. We do not know for certain when Jesus will return, so we need to be ready every single day as we eagerly await His coming for us.

The words from Matthew Henry's commentary are also very good advice for the wise: "Therefore every day and every hour we must be ready, and not off our watch any day in the year, or any hour in the day" (M. H. Volume 5, Page 372).

# Appendix 7 – Signs of Christ's Coming

Many modern Bible teachers and students believe that the rebirth of the nation of Israel represents the budding of the *fig tree* that Jesus described to His disciples as he sat on the Mount of Olives, and we are living in the generation that won't pass away before He returns.

> *Verily I say unto you, this generation shall not pass, till all these things be fulfilled.* (Mat 24:34 – KJV)

With Israel becoming a nation in 1948, we have been alerted that the Lord's return is fast approaching. Jesus also told his disciples a second sign to look for in the parable of Noah:

> *As it was in the days of Noah,*
> *so it will be at the coming of the Son of Man.*
> (Mat 24:37 – NIV)

Here the Lord is telling the Church that just prior to His return, things will be the same as they were back in Noah's day. This pictures life going on right up until the day that the rapture occurs, and the judgments of God are suddenly released upon the earth. A careful study of Genesis 6 will alert the reader to the fact that living in these end times is almost parallel to the time before the flood. The world has become a great cesspool of corruption, violence, sex, drugs, idolatry, witchcraft and other perversions. Reading the account in Genesis is like reading today's newspaper or listening to the daily news.

In the Lord's parable concerning Noah, Jesus was also giving us a second important sign that His return is drawing very near. Several years ago a famous comet passed though our solar system and it was hailed at the most watched comet of all times.

## Sign of Christ's Coming

April 8, 1997

**Comet Hale-Bopp Over New York City**
**Credit and Copyright:** J. Sivo
http://antwrp.gsfc.nasa.gov/apod/ap970408.html

"What's that point of light above the World Trade Center? It's Comet Hale-Bopp! Both faster than a speeding bullet and able to "leap" tall buildings in its single <u>orbit,</u> Comet Hale-Bopp is also bright enough to be seen even over the glowing lights of one of the world's premier cities. In the foreground lies the East River, while much of New York City's Lower Manhattan can be seen between the river and the comet."

*But as the days of Noe were, so shall also the coming*
*of the Son of man be. For as in the days that were before*
*the flood they were eating and drinking, marrying and*
*giving in marriage, until the day that Noe entered into*
*the ark, And knew not until the flood came, and took*
*them all away; so shall also the coming of the Son of man be.*
(Mat 24:37-39 – KJV)

These words from our wonderful Lord have several applications about the generation that is about to witness the Lord's return.

Seas Lifted Up
Throughout the Old Testament, the time of the coming Tribulation period is described as the time when the "seas have lifted up," and also as coming in as a "flood" (please see Jeremiah 51:42, Hosea 5:10, Daniel 11:40 and Psalm 93:3-4 for just a few examples).

This is a direct parallel to the time of Noah when the Great Flood of water came to wipe out every living creature, except for righteous Noah and his family, and the pairs of animals that God spared. While God said that He would never flood the earth again with water, the coming Judgment will be by fire (see II Peter 3:10). The book of Revelation shows that billions of people are about to perish in the terrible time that lies just ahead (see Revelation 6:8 and 9:15).

2 Witnesses
A guiding principle of God is to establish a matter based upon the witness of two or more:

> *A matter must be established by the testimony of two or three witnesses.* (Deuteronomy 19:15 – NIV)

In 1994, God was able to get the attention of mankind when Comet Shoemaker-Levy crashed into Jupiter on the 9th of Av (on the Jewish calendar). Interestingly, this Comet was named after the "two" witnesses who first discovered it.

In 1995, "two" more astronomers also discovered another comet. It was called Comet Hale-Bopp and it reached its closest approach to planet Earth on March 23, 1997. It has been labeled as the most widely viewed comet in the history of mankind.

Scientists have determined that Comet Hale-Bopp's orbit brought it to our solar system 4,465 years ago (see Notes 1 and 2 below). In other words, the comet made its appearance near Earth in 1997 and also in 2468 BC. Remarkably, this comet preceded the Great Flood by 120 years! God warned Noah of this in Genesis 6:3:

> *My Spirit shall not strive with man forever, for he is indeed flesh; yet his days shall be one hundred and twenty years.*

Days of Noah

What does all of this have to do with the Lord's return? Noah was born around 2948 BC, and Genesis 7:11, tells us that the Flood took place when Noah was 600, or in 2348 BC.

Remember, our Lord told us: ***"As it was in the days of Noah, so it will be at the coming of the Son of Man"*** (Matthew 24:37 – NIV).

In the original Greek, it is saying: ***"exactly like"*** it was, so it will be when He comes (see Strong's #5618).

During the days of Noah, Comet Hale-Bopp arrived on the scene as a harbinger of the Great Flood. Just as this same comet appeared before the Flood, could its arrival again in 1997 be a sign that God's final Judgment, also known as the time of great tribulation, is about to begin?

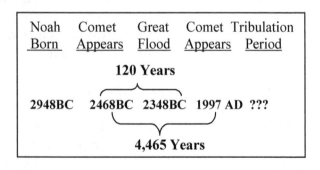

| Noah Born | Comet Appears | Great Flood | Comet Appears | Tribulation Period |
|---|---|---|---|---|
| | | **120 Years** | | |
| 2948BC | 2468BC | 2348BC | 1997 AD | ??? |
| | | **4,465 Years** | | |

Comet Hale-Bopp arrived 120 years before the Flood as a warning to mankind. Only righteous Noah heeded God's warning and built the ark, as God instructed. By faith, Noah was obedient to God and, as a result, saved himself and his family from destruction.

Remember, Jesus told us His return would be preceded by great heavenly signs: *"And there shall be signs in the sun, and in the moon, and in the stars; and upon the earth distress of nations, with perplexity; the sea and the waves roaring..."* (Luke 21:25)

Just as this large comet appeared as a 120-year warning to Noah, its arrival in 1997 tells us that Jesus is getting ready to return again. Is this the **"Sign"** to which Jesus referred?

---

Jesus was asked 3 questions by the disciples:
*Tell us, (1) when shall these things be (the destruction of the city of Jerusalem), and   (2) what shall be the **sign** of thy coming, and (3) of the end of the world?* (Matthew 24:3)

---

## Sign of Christ's Coming

The **first** question had to do with events that were fulfilled in 70 AD. The **third** question has to do with the future time at the very end of the age.

The **second** question; however, has to do with the time of Christ's second coming. Jesus answered this second question in His description of the days of Noah found in Matthew 24:33-39:

> *(33)So likewise ye, when ye shall see all these things, know that it is near, even at the doors. (34) Verily I say unto you, This generation shall not pass, till all these things be fulfilled. (35) Heaven and earth shall pass away, but my words shall not pass away. (36) But of that day and hour knoweth no man, no, not the angels of heaven, but my Father only. (37) **But as the days of Noe were, so shall also the coming of the Son***

> *of man be.* [(38)] *For as in the days that were before the flood they were eating and drinking, marrying and giving in marriage, until the day that Noe entered into the ark,* [(39)] *And knew not until the flood came, and took them all away; so shall also the coming of the Son of man be.*

Jesus is telling us that the *sign* of His coming will be as it was during the days of Noah. As Comet Hale-Bopp was a sign to the people in Noah's day, its arrival in 1997 may be a sign that Jesus is coming back again soon. Comet Hale-Bopp could be the very sign Jesus was referring to, which would announce His return for His faithful.

Remember, Jesus said, *"exactly as it was in the days of Noah, so will it be when He returns."* The appearance of Comet Hale-Bopp in 1997 is a strong indication that the tribulation period is about to begin, but before then, Jesus is coming for His bride!

**Keep looking up! Jesus is coming again very soon!**
As Noah prepared for the destruction God warned him approximately 120 years before the Flood, Jesus has given mankind final warnings that we are living in the generation that will witness His return. We do not know how long a generation may be. For this reason we need to be wise like Noah and prepare by always remembering our Lord's instructions:

### Watch and Pray

> *(34) And take heed to yourselves, lest at any time your hearts be overcharged with surfeiting, and drunkenness, and cares of this life, and so that day come upon you unawares. (35) For as a snare shall it come on all them that dwell on the face of the whole earth. (36)* ***Watch ye therefore, and pray always, that ye may be accounted worthy to escape all these things that shall come to pass, and to stand before the Son of man.*** (Luke 21:34-36–KJV)

## Footnotes to Appendix 7

(1) The original orbit of Comet Hale-Bopp was calculated to be approximately 265 years by engineer George Sanctuary in his article, *Three Craters In Israel*, published on 3/31/01 found at: http://www.gsanctuary.com/3craters.html#3c_r13

Comet Hale-Bopp's orbit around the time of the Flood changed from 265 years to about 4,200 years. Because the plane of the comet's orbit is perpendicular to the earth's orbital plane (ecliptic), Mr. Sanctuary noted: "A negative time increment was used for this simulation…to back the comet away from the earth…. past Jupiter… and then out of the solar system. The simulation suggests that the past-past orbit had a very eccentric orbit with a period of only 265 years. When the comet passed Jupiter (*around 2203BC)* its orbit was deflected upward, coming down near the earth 15 months later with the comet's period changed from 265 years to about (*4,200)* years." (*added text for clarity*)

(2) Don Yeomans, with NASA's Jet Propulsion Laboratory, made the following observations regarding the comet's orbit: "By integrating the above orbit forward and backward in time until the comet leaves the planetary system and then referring the osculating orbital elements…the following orbital periods result:

> Original orbital period before entering planetary system = 4200 years. Future orbital period after exiting the planetary system = 2380 years."

> This analysis can be found at:
> http://www2.jpl.nasa.gov/comet/ephemjpl6.html

Based upon the above two calculations we have the following:

**265 [a] + 4,200 [b] = 4,465 Years**

**1997 AD – 4,465 Years = 2468 BC = Hale Bopp arrived**

(a) Orbit period calculated by George Sanctuary before deflection around 2203 BC.
(b) Orbit period calculated by Don Yeomans after 1997 visit.

---

## LEAVE A REVIEW

Now that you have finished this book, we encourage you to take the time to go to Amazon.com to rate and review this work to let people know what you thought about it and how this book has been a blessing to you. Since Jesus is returning soon, it is important to help others get prepared. Leaving a review on Amazon is one way to facilitate this.

# The Advocate

*My little children, these things I write to you, so that you may not sin. And if anyone sins, we have an Advocate with the Father, Jesus Christ the righteous.*
(1Jo 2:1)

Image of the Advocate by Steve Creitz, www.ProphecyArt.com
Please see the **Supplemental Articles** section of our website:
www.ProphecyCountdown.com, for more on our Advocate.

# Special Invitation

We hope that this book helps you see how very important it is to know and love Jesus Christ before it's too late. If you have never been saved before, would you like to be saved? The Bible shows that it's simple to be saved...

- **Realize you are a sinner.**
  *As it is written, There is none righteous, no, not one:*
  (Romans 3:10 – KJV)
  *For there is no difference. For all have sinned, and come short of the glory of God;* (Romans 3:22-23– KJV)

- **Realize you CAN NOT save yourself.**
  *But we are all as an unclean thing, and all our righteousness are as filthy rags;* (Isaiah 64:6 – KJV)
  *Not by works of righteousness which we have done, but according to his mercy he saved us,* (Titus 3:5– KJV)

- **Realize that Jesus Christ died on the cross to pay for your sins.**
  *Who his own self bare our sins in his own body on the tree,* (I Peter 2:24 – KJV)
  *Unto him that loved us, and washed us from our sins in his own blood,* (Revelation 1:5– KJV)

- **Simply by faith receive Jesus Christ as your personal Saviour.**
  *But as many as received him, to them gave he power to become the sons of God, even to them that believe on his name* (John 1:12– KJV)
  *'Sirs, what must I do to be saved?' And they said, 'Believe on the Lord Jesus Christ, and thou shalt be saved, and thy house.'* (Acts 16:30-31 – KJV)

**WOULD YOU LIKE TO BE SAVED?**

If you would like to be saved, believe on the Lord Jesus Christ (Act 16:31) right now by making this acknowledgment in your heart:

> Lord Jesus, I know that I am a sinner, and unless You save me, I am lost. I thank You for dying for me at Calvary. By faith I come to You now, Lord, the best way I know how, and ask You to save me. I believe that God raised You from the dead and acknowledge You as my personal Saviour.

If you believed on the Lord, this is the most important decision of your life. You are now saved by the precious blood of Jesus Christ, which was shed for you and your sins. Now that you have believed on Jesus as your personal Saviour, you will want to find a Church where you can be baptized as your first act of obedience, and where the Word of God is taught so you can continue to grow in your faith. Ask the Holy Spirit to help you as you read the Bible to learn all that God has for your life.

Also, see the Reference Notes and Bibliography section of this book, where you will find recommended books and websites that will help you on your wonderful journey.

### Endtimes
The Bible indicates that we are living in the final days and Jesus Christ is getting ready to return very soon. This book was written to help people prepare to meet the Lord when He comes. The Word of God indicates that the tribulation period is rapidly approaching and that the Antichrist is getting ready to emerge on the world scene.

Jesus promised His disciples that there is a way to escape the horrible time of testing and persecution that will soon devastate this planet. One of the purposes of this book is to help you get prepared so you will be ready when Jesus Christ returns. We also highly recommend reading *Calling All Overcomers*, which covers the important book of Revelation.

# About the Author

————◇◆◇————

Jim Harman has been a Christian for 41 years. He has diligently studied the Word of God with a particular emphasis on prophecy. Jim has written several books, and the most essential titles are available at www.ProphecyCountdown.com: *Coming Spiritual Earthquake, The Kingdom, Overcomers' Guide To The Kingdom, Calling All Overcomers, Daniel's Prophecies: Unsealed.* All these books may be freely downloaded as PDF files, and they will encourage you to continue *"Looking"* for the blessed hope of the Lord's soon return.

Jim's professional experience included being a Certified Public Accountant (CPA) and a Certified Property Manager (CPM). He had an extensive background in both public accounting and financial management with several well-known national firms.

Jim has been fortunate to have been acquainted with several mature believers who understand and teach the deeper truths of the Bible. It is Jim's strong desire that many will come to realize the importance of seeking the Kingdom and seeking Christ's righteousness as we approach the soon return of our Lord and Saviour Jesus Christ.

The burden of his heart is to see many come to know the joy of Christ's triumph in their life as they become true overcomers, qualified and ready to rule and reign with Christ in the coming Kingdom.

To contact the author for questions, to arrange for speaking engagements or to order multiple copies of this book:

> Jim Harman
> P.O. Box 941612
> Maitland, FL 32794
> JamesTHarman@aol.com

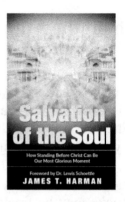

## HOW STANDING BEFORE CHRIST
## CAN BE OUR MOST GLORIOUS MOMENT

The topic of the Judgment Seat of Christ is often neglected by today's modern church.

> *"For we must all appear before the judgment seat of Christ, that each one may receive the things done in the body, according to what he has done, whether good or bad"* (2 Corinthians 5:10).

When Jesus returns, He will review all of our lives to determine whether we have been faithful and obedient doers of His Word. The purpose of this book is to prepare believers so they will be able to hear Him say:

> *"Well done, good and faithful servant....*
> ***Enter into the joy of your lord"*** (Matthew 25:21).

### MUST-READ FOR ALL BELIEVERS

NEW DISCOVERY – LEARN ABOUT
- Difference between the salvation of spirit and soul.
- What Jesus meant by *"take up your cross."*
- How the Word of God can save our souls.
- When the salvation of our soul takes place.
- Sign of Christ's Coming

Download your FREE copy: www.ProphecyCountdown.com

Or from Amazon.com–Available in Paperback and/or Kindle Edition

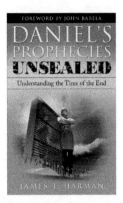

*"Go your way Daniel, because the words are closed up and sealed until the time of the end...none of the wicked will understand, but those who are wise will understand."*
(Daniel 12:9-10)

The Archangel Michael told Daniel that the prophecies would be sealed until the time of the end. Discover how the prophecies in the book of Daniel are being unsealed in the events taking place today.

Since Daniel was told that the wise will understand the message and lead many to righteousness, while the wicked will not grasp its meaning and will continue in their wickedness, it is imperative for everyone living in these end times to diligently examine and attempt to comprehend the vital message Daniel has recorded for us. The wise will diligently search the word of the Lord and ask for wisdom in order to understand God's plan.

When Jesus came the first time, the wise men of the day were aware of His soon arrival and they were actively looking for Him. Today, those who are wise will be passionately sharing this message and helping others prepare. Those doing so will *"shine like the stars forever and ever."*

May the Lord grant us a heart of wisdom to understand the time we are living in so we can prepare for what lies ahead!

Download your FREE copy: www.ProphecyCountdown.com

Or from Amazon.com–Available in Paperback and/or Kindle Edition

An Interpretation of the Song of Solomon
Foreword by John Zajac

**James T. Harman**

God placed the Song of Solomon in the heart of the Bible for a special reason. *Come Away My Beloved* helps reveal that reason in a most enchanting way. In this refreshing commentary you will realize why this ancient love story has perplexed Bible students and commentators down through the ages.

Find out the prophetic importance veiled within the Song's poetic imagery and experience a renewed love for the Lord as you explore one of the most passionate love stories of all time.

Witness the wonderful joys of romance and devotion shared by two young lovers. Discover enduring lessons of virtue and faithfulness, and learn amazing truths that have been hidden within the greatest love Song ever written.

Written almost 3,000 years ago this brilliant Song of love reflects God's desire for every man and woman; not only in their present lives but also in their relationship with Him.

This book will revive your heart with a fervent love for your Saviour. It will also help you prepare for your glorious wedding day when Jesus returns for His devoted bride.

Allow this beautiful story of love and passion to ignite a flame in your heart and let this inspirational Song arouse your heart to join in the impassioned cry with the rest of the bride:

*"Make haste, my beloved, and come quickly…"*

Download your FREE copy: www.ProphecyCountdown.com

Or from Amazon.com–Available in Paperback and/or Kindle Edition

Perplexed by the book of Revelation? Not sure what all the signs, symbols and metaphors really mean? Jim Harman's latest work unravels Apostle John's remarkable revelation of Jesus Christ and what's in store for the inhabitants of planet Earth. This extraordinary commentary is not another cookie-cutter rehash of the popular teachings fostered by the *Left Behind* phenomena so prevalent in today's church.

One of the central messages in the book of Revelation is that God is calling men to be genuine overcomers. Jesus Christ has been sent out from the throne of God to conquer men's hearts so they can also be overcomers.

The purpose of this book is to encourage people to embrace Him as the King of their heart and allow His life to reign in theirs. He wants you to be able to overcome by His mighty power and strength living inside of you just as He overcame for all of us. Jesus will be looking for a faithful remnant qualified to rule and reign with Him when He returns. This book will help you prepare to be the overcomer for which Jesus is looking.

The reader will come away with a new and enlightened understanding of what the last book in God's Word is all about. Understand the book of Revelation and why it is so important for believers living in the last days of the Church age.

Download your FREE copy: www.ProphecyCountdown.com

Or from Amazon.com–Available in Paperback and/or Kindle Edition

Once a person is saved, the number one priority should be seeking entrance into the Kingdom through the salvation of their soul. It is pictured as a runner in a race seeking a prize represented by a crown that will last forever.

The salvation of the soul and entrance into the coming Kingdom are only achieved through much testing and the trial of one's faith. If you are going through difficulty, then REJOICE:

> *"Blessed is the man who perseveres under trial, because when he has stood the test, he will receive the crown of life that God has promised to those who love Him."* (James 1:12)

The "Traditional" teaching on the "THE KINGDOM" has taken the Church captive into believing all Christians will rule and reign with Christ no matter if they have lived faithful and obedient lives, or if they have been slothful and disobedient with the talents God has given them. Find out the important Truth before Jesus Christ returns.

## MUST READING FOR EVERY CHRISTIAN

Jesus Christ is returning for His faithful overcoming followers. Don't miss the opportunity of ruling and reigning with Christ in the coming KINGDOM!

Download your FREE copy:  www.ProphecyCountdown.com

Or from Amazon.com–Available in Paperback and/or Kindle Edition

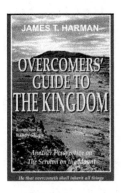

Get ready to climb back up the Mountain to listen to Christ's teachings once again. Though you may have read this great Sermon on the Mount many times, discover exciting promises that many have missed.

The purpose of this book is to help Christians be the Overcomers that Jesus wants them to be and to help them gain their own entrance in the coming Kingdom. Learn what seeking the Kingdom of God is all about and be among the chosen few who will "enter into" the coming Kingdom. *"Whoever hears these sayings of Mine, and does them, I will liken him to a wise man who built his house upon the rock."* (Mat 7:24)

Also learn about:
- The link between Beatitudes and Fruit of the Spirit
- What the "law of Christ" really is
- The critical importance of the "Lord's prayer"
- How to be an Overcomer
- THE SIGN of Christ's soon Coming
- A new song entitled: LOOKING FOR THE SON which has the message of how vitally important it is to be Watching for the Lord's return and the consequences to those who are not looking.

Download your FREE copy: www.ProphecyCountdown.com

Or from Amazon.com–Available in Paperback and/or Kindle Edition

# *LOOKING FOR THE SON*

### Lyrics by Jim Harman
### Listen to this Song on the Home Page of Prophecy Countdown

| Lyric | Scripture |
|---|---|
| *There's a fire burning in my heart* | Luke 24:32 |
| *Yearning for the Lord to come,* | Rev. 22:17, Mat. 6:33 |
| *and His Kingdom come to start* | |
| *Soon He'll come.....so enter the narrow gate* | Lk. 21:34-36,Mat.7:13 |
| *Even though you mock me now...* | II Peter 3:4 |
| *He'll come to set things straight* | |
| *Watch how I'll leave in the twinkling of an eye* | I Corinthians 15:52 |
| *Don't be surprised when I go up in the sky* | Revelation 3:10 |
| | |
| *There's a fire burning in my heart* | Luke 24:32 |
| *Yearning for my precious Lord* | Revelation 22:17 |
| *And His Kingdom come to start* | Revelation 20:4-6 |
| | |
| *Your love of this world, has forsaken His* | I John 2:15 |
| *It leaves me knowing that you could have had it all* | Revelation 21:7 |
| *Your love of this world, was oh so reckless* | Revelation 3:14-22 |
| *I can't help thinking* | Philippians 1:3-6 |
| *You would have had it all* | Revelation 21:7 |
| | |
| *Looking for the Son* | Titus 2:13, Luke 21:36 |
| *(Tears are gonna fall, not looking for the Son)* | Matthew 25:10-13 |
| *You had His holy Word in your hand* | II Timothy 3:16 |
| *(You're gonna wish you had listened to me)* | Jeremiah 25:4-8 |
| *And you missed it...for your self* | Matthew 22:11-14 |
| *(Tears are gonna fall, not looking for the Son)* | Matthew 25:10-13 |
| | |
| *Brother, I have a story to be told* | Habakkuk 2:2 |
| *It's the only one that's true* | John 3:16-17 |
| *And it should've made your heart turn* | II Peter 3:9 |
| *Remember me when I rise up in the air* | I Corinthians 15:52 |
| *Leaving your home down here* | I Corinthians 15:52 |
| *For true Treasures beyond compare* | Matthew 6:20 |
| *Your love of this world, has forsaken His* | I John 2:15 |
| *It leaves me knowing that you could have had it all* | Revelation 21:7 |
| *Your love of this world, was oh so reckless* | Revelation 3:14-22 |
| *I can't help thinking* | Philippians 1:3-6 |
| *You would have had it all* | Revelation 21:7 |

*(Lyrics in parentheses represent background vocals)*
(CONTINUED)

| Lyric | Scripture |
|---|---|
| *Looking for the Son* | Titus 2:13, Lk. 21:36 |
| *(Tears are gonna fall, not looking for the Son)* | Matthew 25:10-13 |
| *You had His holy Word in your hand* | II Timothy 3:16 |
| *(You're gonna wish you had listened to me)* | Jeremiah 25:4-8 |
| *And you lost it...for your self* | Matthew 22:11-14 |
| *(Tears are gonna fall, not looking for the Son)* | Matthew 25:10-13 |
| *You would have had it all* | Revelation 21:7 |
| *Looking for the Son* | Titus 2:13, Lk. 21:36 |
| *You had His holy Word in your hand* | II Timothy 3:16 |
| *But you missed it... for your self* | Matthew 22:11-14 |
| | |
| *Lov'n the world....not the open door* | I Jn. 2:15, Rev. 4:1 |
| *Down the broad way... blind to what life's really for* | Matthew 7:13-14 |
| *Turn around now...while there still is time* | I Jn. 1:9, II Pet. 3:9 |
| *Learn your lesson now or you'll reap just what you sow* | Galatians 6:7 |

*(You're gonna wish you had listened to me)*
*You would have had it all*
*(Tears are gonna fall, not looking for the Son)*
*You would have had it all*
*(You're gonna wish you had listened to me)*
*It all, it all, it all*
*(Tears are gonna fall, not looking for the Son)*

*You would have had it all*
*(You're gonna wish you had listened to me)*
*Looking for the Son*
*(Tears are gonna fall, not looking for the Son)*
*You had His holy Word in your hand*
*(You're gonna wish you had listened to me)*
*And you missed it...for your self*
*(Tears are gonna fall, not looking for the Son)*

*You would have had it all*
*(You're gonna wish you had listened to me)*
*Looking for the Son*
*(Tears are gonna fall, not looking for the Son)*
*You had His holy Word in your hand*
*(You're gonna wish you had listened to me)*
*But you missed it*
*You missed it*
*You missed it*
*You missed it....for your self*

**Scripture Summary**
Jeremiah 25:4-8
Habakkuk 2:2
Matthew 6:20
Matthew 6:33
Matthew 7:13
Matthew 22:11-14
Matthew 25:10-13
Luke 21:34-36
Luke 24:332
John 3:16-17
I Corinthians 15:52
Galatians 6:7
Philippians 1:3-6
II Timothy 3:16
Titus 2:13
II Peter 3:9
II Peter 3:4
I John 1:9
I John 2:15
Revelation 3:10
Revelation 3:14-22
Revelation 4:1
Revelation 20:4-6
Revelation 21:7
Revelation 22:17

(See www.ProphecyCountdown.com for more information)

# The Day of the Lord is Near!

## The Coming Spiritual Earthquake

### by James T. Harman

"The Message presented in this book is greatly needed to awaken believers to the false ideas many have when it comes to the Rapture. I might have titled it: THE RAPTURE EARTH-QUAKE!"
*Ray Brubaker* - God's News Behind the News

"If I am wrong, anyone who follows the directions given in this book will be better off spiritually. If I am right, they will be among the few to escape the greatest spiritual calamity of the ages."
*Jim Harman* - Author

**MUST READING FOR EVERY CHRISTIAN!**
**HURRY! BEFORE IT IS TOO LATE!**

CPSIA information can be obtained
at www.ICGtesting.com
Printed in the USA
BVHW050738300423
663287BV00014B/852